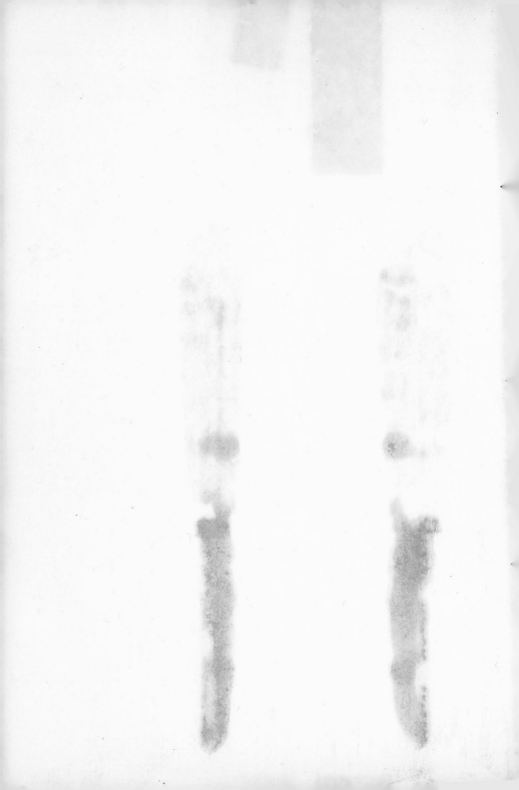

YOUR MONEY:
HOW TO
MAKE IT
WORK HARDER
THAN YOU DO

Richard Phalon

YOUR

MONEY:

How to Make It Work Harder Than You Do

ST. MARTIN'S PRESS   New York

Copyright © 1979 by Richard Phalon
All rights reserved. For information, write:
St. Martin's Press, Inc., 175 Fifth Ave., New York, N.Y. 10010.
Manufactured in the United States of America
Library of Congress Catalog Card Number: 78-21363

Library of Congress Cataloging in Publication Data

Phalon, Richard.
    Your money.

    1. Finance, Personal.   I. Title.
HG179.P45   332′.024   78-21363
ISBN 0-312-89822-3

To my mother and father

CONTENTS

HOW TO MAKE MONEY IN REAL ESTATE

HOW TO MANAGE YOUR INVESTMENTS

HOW TO MANAGE YOUR INCOME TAX

Acknowledgments

This book has been a collaborative venture. I am grateful to everyone who, over the years, has taken time out to point me in the right research direction. Most of those who can be mentioned by name have been cited in the text. That doesn't mean I am any less grateful to those who prefer not to be mentioned, including D. O'B., who provided much technical assistance. I owe thanks to George Brounoff, a bond trader's bond trader and one of Wall Street's most literate men, who read the section on investing; to Eli Mason and Robert Parks of Mason & Co., accountant's accountants both, who read the section on taxes; and to Miriam Harvey Phalon, a proofreader's proofreader, who read the entire book. The opinions are my own, but many picked up errors in manuscript that would have left me stripped bare by my readers.

STRATEGY

Chapter 1

Your Money Plan

Charles Dickens, who knew firsthand the ignominy of debtors' prison and other rack-rent pressures of Victoria's England, had Micawber say it all: "Annual income twenty pounds, annual expenditures nineteen nineteen six, result happiness. Annual expenditure, twenty pounds, ought and six, result misery."

This is not Victoria's England, but there is plenty of misery around. The twin scourges of inflation and the progressive income tax have left many of us with the panicky feeling that we've got absolutely no control over where our money goes, and no wonder. Partly because the tax structure is graded so steeply, a person who was in the 25 percent tax bracket 10 years ago is in the 35 percent bracket today. Every time you get a pay raise you hope will keep you abreast of the cost of living, you find the Internal Revenue Service digging deeper into your pocket. More is less.

The treadmill churns away at such a bewildering rate that Cunningham & Walsh Inc.'s continuing survey for its advertising clients of the impact of change on young families is rife with examples like this:

"I wish I did have something set aside for my kids to go to college just in case they wanted to," one father told the interviewers, "but this doesn't fit into my personal financial plans right now. I cannot afford to tie the money up."

The same man was almost sick over the rise in housing costs. "I literally can't afford to buy the house I used to live in," he said.

Micawber had it right. Even a small surplus helps to ease some of the anxieties most of us feel about money. With the strategies you'll find in this book (and a little bit of luck), you'll be able to minimize the tax bite and manage yourself into a surplus.

The surplus is vital to working out a master plan that should include: (1) a comparatively modest savings account to cover such small emergencies as an unexpected dental bill or a new set of snows for the car; (2) a somewhat large higher-yielding cash equivalent reserve to protect yourself against big emergencies—a job loss, for example; (3) enough life, medical, and maybe disability insurance to protect you and your family against catastrophe; and (4) a balanced investment portfolio that will help you put the kids through college, cushion your retirement years, and achieve whatever other financial goals you've set for yourself.

Any idiot can make lists. Real life is full of pitfalls. Maybe you can learn from other people's mistakes. Peter M. Mazonas, for example, head of the Bank of America's financial counseling service, has discovered that corporate executives—like the very rich—really are not so very different from you and me.

In the years that he has been helping executives learn how to handle their own money, Mazonas has found that the brass makes over and over again many of the same mistakes that we amateur managers do.

The most common error is a tendency to be "too busy" to do any financial planning on a regular basis. Many people, the Bank of America vice-president contends, take the attitude "there's money in the checking account, so everything must be all right." Then there's an eruption—an overlooked insurance bill, an unexpectedly high tax bill. "That's crisis management," Mazonas told me in an interview for *The New York Times*. "People will go for weeks or months without doing anything about personal problems that need regular attention."

Problems that seem to jump out of the woodwork are the reason why the keystone of what might be called the Micawber money plan is a two-pronged cash reserve—one in a regular savings account, the other in such cash equivalents as the Treasury bills, money market funds and the like discussed in the next chapter. How big should those reserves be?

The conventional wisdom among financial planners is three to six months net pay. To some degree, the answer to the question is totally subjective. Some people just feel more comfortable with a solid chunk of cash ready to hand, like the Third Avenue saloon keeper I used to know—Hibernian, of course—who always kept a couple of grand stashed behind the register in case he needed the restorative of a flying trip back to the old country.

There ought to be enough ready cash around to cover at least a month's worth of bills, but that, too, depends on variables such as your company's sick pay policy, the kind of medical insurance you've got, and maybe the size of the pension you draw.

I think it is bad management to keep too much money tied up in a regular savings account where the return (5 percent, maybe 5.25 percent) doesn't even begin to match the rate of inflation. Your emergency fund is literally withering away. It's possible to have too much money in the bank. It's also possible to have too much—or too little—life insurance.

The best way of thinking through the deployment of your assets is to figure out your net worth—i.e., work out a balance sheet of your assets and liabilities. In essence, you are taking a snapshot of where you are now. This is an invaluable planning tool that can help you decide where to go next. Perhaps you should stop renting and buy a house or a condominium, a move that could cut your taxes and build your equity base. Maybe taking tax losses on a couple of stocks that turned out to be clinkers will help you fatten your investment return.

As you will note from the sample balance sheet supplied by the Bank of America NT & SA, a net worth statement is an inventory of what you own and what you owe. Putting together such a statement on the same day once a year is a good way to keep tabs on how you're doing.

What is your net worth and what are your objectives? If they include early retirement from a job you loathe, starting a business of your own, or buying a home, there is no better time to put your financial plan into action than now. The longer you wait, the tougher it gets. A person who invests $20 a month at age 25, at an average interest rate of 7 percent a year, can accumulate about $50,000 by age 65. If you put off investing until age 35, it would take $40 a month to accumulate $50,000. At age 55, it would take about $305 a month to attain the same goal.

Where is the $20—or $40 a month—going to come from? Squeezing a surplus out of the only earnings stream most of us have, the paycheck, is a grungy prospect at best because it's subtractive. It means giving something up, and that something is often either pleasurable or a soul-pampering convenience—a good brand of Scotch, or a taxi when it rains.

One standard money management tool, the net worth statement, has told you where you stand. Still another management tool—a cash flow statement—can help you figure out where your money is going. And once you know where the cash is going, you should be able to figure out how to put some of it to more productive use. The Bank of America income

BALANCE SHEET

_____ ____, 19___

ASSETS   Everything you own with cash value.

CASH   Money you have on hand. Include cash at home, today's checking and savings account balances. $ _____

STOCKS, BONDS, OTHER SECURITIES   U.S. Savings Bonds, Treasury issues, other money market and stock market investments. Check your records for documentation of current holdings. Current market value for some types of securities may be found in newspaper financial pages; for others, contact your broker. $ _____

CASH SURRENDER VALUE LIFE INSURANCE   Investment or equity built up in your whole or straight life insurance policy; not face value. (Term life insurance has no cash surrender value.) Find the cash surrender value from the chart on your policy. $ _____

ACCOUNTS RECEIVABLE   Money owed to you for goods and/or services. Check your files for bills outstanding. $ _____

NOTES RECEIVABLE   Money owed to you and documented by promissory notes. Check your records for the balance of any note due you. $ _____

REBATES/REFUNDS   Money owed to you for refundable deposits, sales or tax refunds or rebates. Check your files for receipts and current 1040 income tax form. $ _____

AUTOS/OTHER VEHICLES   Trucks, trailers, mobile homes, motorcycles, campers, boats and airplanes. Vehicle dealers and some libraries carry special price books such as the Kelley Blue Book for new and used automobiles. If no published information is available, dealers may be able to tell you the current market value. $ _____

REAL ESTATE   Any land and/or structures affixed to land. Also, legal rights you may have to resources in the land: growing crops, water, minerals, etc. For an estimate of the current market value, you may contact a local real estate agent or hire a professional appraiser. $ _____

VESTED PENSION   Nonforfeitable rights to benefits you accumulate after a certain time under your employer's pension plan. To find the current amount of your benefits, you must submit a written request to your employer or plan administrator. $ _____

KEOGH OR INDIVIDUAL RETIREMENT ACCOUNT   Available to those without employer pension plans or the self-employed. Record your account balance. $ _____

OTHER ASSETS   Any property other than real estate that has cash value, estimated in terms of what it is worth today. To find an item's value, check classified ads for comparable items or get estimates from dealers or special appraisers.

Home furnishings/household goods/appliances $ _____

Hobby/sports equipment $ _____

Art/antiques/collections/ jewelry/furs $ _____

Trade/professional tools and equipment $ _____

Livestock/pets for show or breeding $ _____

Trusts/patents/memberships interest in estate $ _____

Interest in business/farm/commercial operation investment club. (Any whole or part ownership.) $ _____

TOTAL ASSETS $ _____

LIABILITIES   What you owe; your debts.

ACCOUNTS PAYABLE   Total balance of what you owe today on bills for goods and services (such as doctor bills) and credit card and store accounts. A credit card company or store usually lists the account's total balance due on the monthly statement mailed to you. If you do not have these records, contact the credit departments of firms where you have accounts. $ _____

CONTRACTS PAYABLE   Total remaining balance on installment credit contracts for goods such as a car, furniture, appliances, or services of someone working for you under contract. To figure the total amount due, multiply your monthly payment by the number of months remaining on the contract. $ _____

NOTES PAYABLE   Total balance due on cash loans, both secured and unsecured. Contact the office where you received the loan if you don't have these figures. $ _____

TAXES   Federal and state income or property taxes due as of today (including any past due taxes). Do not list property taxes if they are automatically included with your mortgage payments. Self-employed people should include any Social Security taxes due. Check your income tax or property tax statements. $ _____

REAL ESTATE LOANS   Balance you owe on deeds of trust (mortgages) on your property. Contact the office where you received the loan if you don't have these figures. Also list any liens on property that you are liable for and must pay. $ _____

OTHER LIABILITIES   Court-ordered judgments of payments you must make, lawsuit settlements, past due accounts, etc. $ _____

TOTAL LIABILITIES $ _____

CONTINGENT LIABILITIES   Debts you may or may not come to owe sometime in the future. If you cosigned a note and the other signer doesn't pay, you may be responsible for paying the debt. If a suit is pending against you, you may be liable to pay a settlement. $ _____

NET WORTH   Your assets less your liabilities.

ASSETS $ _____

LESS LIABILITIES

NET WORTH $ _____

**To check your figures, make sure:
Assets=Liabilities+Net Worth**

INCOME AND EXPENSE STATEMENT

From _____, 19__ to _____ , 19 __

INCOME Money you receive for your use.

GROSS SALARY/WAGES $ _____

LESS DEDUCTIONS Federal and state income tax, FICA, unemployment compensation.
–$ _____

    TAKE-HOME PAY $ _____

SPOUSE OR OTHER GROSS SALARY/WAGES $ _____

LESS DEDUCTIONS –$ _____

    TAKE-HOME PAY $ _____

COMMISSIONS, TIPS, BONUSES $ _____

NET PROFIT FROM BUSINESS, FARM, TRADE, PROFESSION $ _____

INTEREST OR DIVIDENDS FROM SAVINGS, STOCKS, BONDS, OTHER SECURITIES, NOTES $ _____

NET PROFIT FROM SALE OF ASSETS $ _____

NET PROFIT FROM RENTAL PROPERTY $ _____

INCOME FROM ALIMONY/CHILD SUPPORT/ MAINTENANCE (Court ordered.)

REFUNDS/REBATES $ _____

CASH GIFTS $ _____

OTHER INCOME
  Social Security benefits $ _____

  Pensions, annuities $ _____

  Veterans benefits $ _____

  Unemployment benefits $ _____

  Disability benefits $ _____

  Life insurance benefits $ _____

  Income from trusts $ _____

  Royalties/residuals $ _____

    TOTAL INCOME $ _____

TOTAL INCOME $ _____

LESS TOTAL EXPENSES (FIXED AND VARIABLE) $ _____

Amount available for savings investments or debt payment $ _____

FIXED EXPENSES Payments you must make, usually set by written agreement, at regular times for set amounts.

RENT OR MORTGAGE PAYMENTS Include property tax and insurance if automatically included in payment. $ _____

OTHER REAL ESTATE PAYMENT Second mortgage, home improvement loan (if secured by home), vacation home, storage rental, homeowner association fees. $ _____

INCOME TAXES Federal and state taxes due in addition to withholding taxes; past taxes. $ _____

PROPERTY TAXES If not part of house payment. $ _____

OTHER TAXES Gift or estate taxes. $ _____

INSTALLMENT CONTRACT PAYMENTS Fixed payments made at regular intervals over specific time periods for purchase of vehicles, mobile home, furniture, appliances, etc. $ _____

PERSONAL PROPERTY LEASE PAYMENTS Auto, furniture, equipment. $ _____

INSURANCE Real property (fire, liability, theft, etc., if not included in house payment), personal property (homeowner's, renter's, auto), life, health, other. $ _____

REGULAR PAYMENTS TO OTHERS Alimony, child support, maintenance. $ _____

REGULAR CONTRIBUTIONS Church, charities, etc. $ _____

DUES Union, club and other memberships. $ _____

TOTAL FIXED EXPENSES $ _____

VARIABLE EXPENSES Regular expenses that may fluctuate from month to month or year to year.

UTILITIES Gas, electricity, heating, fuel, phone, water, cable TV, garbage. $ _____

CHARGE ACCOUNTS Store account and credit card payments. $ _____

MEDICAL/DENTAL Drugs and treatment not covered by insurance. $ _____

TRANSPORTATION Car operating expenses (gas, oil, repairs, servicing), parking, public transportation. $ _____

HOUSEHOLD MAINTENANCE/REPAIR Gardening, cleaning, house/appliance repairs (material, labor). $ _____

CHILD CARE Day care, nursery school, housekeeper, babysitter. $ _____

FOOD Groceries, nonfood items in supermarket bill. $ _____

PERSONAL MAINTENANCE Clothing, laundry, barber, beauty salon, health and beauty products. $ _____

SELF-IMPROVEMENT/EDUCATION Books, magazines, newspapers, seminars, lessons, tuition, room and board away from home. $ _____

RECREATION/ENTERTAINMENT Restaurants, movies, sports, vacations, weekends, parties, etc. $ _____

TOTAL VARIABLE EXPENSES $ _____

TOTAL EXPENSES (FIXED AND VARIABLE) $ _____

and expense statement is a start. To see where it takes you, though, you're going to need decent research material.

Pull out all of your canceled checks from last year, together with credit card statements, charge account billings and any other records that will help to give you a fix on how you've been spending your money. You can reinforce the evidence by keeping tabs for the next couple of months or so on every cent you spend. A pocket notebook is an invaluable aid. Jot it all down. Be particularly vigilant in ferreting out "leaks"—checks written to cash that often get pushed across the counter of your grocer, liquor dealer or some other friendly neighborhood banker late of a Saturday afternoon.

There are a couple of points to the exercise. One is to figure out where the fat is. Most budgets are marbled with flab that can be turned into financial muscle. Maybe the size of the American Express billings suggest you should be eating more Saturday night dinners at home. Can you cut your insurance bill by searching out cheap group term coverage through a fraternal group (see Chapters 7 and 8)? Can you trim your day-to-day expenses by substituting things that cost less but do the same job—a slipcover, say, instead of a new sofa?

Are there economies to be had in doing yourself some of the things you've been paying others to do? Why not learn how to handle your own oil changes and tune-ups instead of putting the car into the repair shop? Do you keep an eye out for supermarket "specials," and seasonal sales on clothing and household linen "white sales"? Set yourself some realistic goals and try to stick to them. Maybe you can trim your clothing bill from $1,000 to $600 a year. If you spend $300 of the new allotment, remember that you've got only another $300 to spend over the rest of the year.

You won't have any trouble finding some place to channel the savings. Depending on what your net worth statement looks like, they should go into your emergency or cash equivalent reserves, or some longer term form of investment. Looking for ways to generate even a small Micawberish surplus ("happiness") is the prime objective of your cash flow study. But the study is also a planning tool, a tool that can help you take some of the panic out of life by anticipating big ticket expenditures before they fall due.

The big ticket budget wreckers fall into two categories: regular expenditures at regular intervals (real estate taxes, life and automobile insurance premiums, for example); and irregular amounts of cash spent at irregular intervals. Clothing and household furnishings are a good example of the latter.

Checking over the cash flow might show that you've got to get up $400 in real estate taxes every quarter, two semi-annual payments of $200 each on your life insurance, and a $400 payment on the automobile insurance next month. Let's say the study also shows that you spent $600 last year on such major impulse items as clothing and home furnishings. All of that adds up to a total of $3,000 a year— $250 a month or about $58 a week.

Set up a special savings account, and credit it on whatever regular basis best fits your pay period. A revolving fund of that kind is the best way to deal with big ticket items. Unless you budget consciously for them, once or twice a year charges tend to slip out of mind. When they do, you've got to scramble to meet them. That's the hard way. The easy way is to anticipate them.

The set aside approach can be made to fit many expenses that fall within reasonably predictable parameters. Some of the items which fall in that category (besides all forms of insurance, real estate taxes and clothing) are: minor home and automobile maintenance, vacations, and such personal care costs as barbers, hairdressers and cosmetics. Utility costs tend to fluctuate with the season, but they too can be averaged out in your revolving fund account. The idea is to smooth out the spending side of the equation—in short, to plan things better so you won't have to invade your savings to meet regular living expenses.

There are ways of helping yourself on the income side of the equation, too. Saving has to be automatized. It should be as metronomic a charge against your earnings as the telephone bill or a mortgage payment. Payroll deduction plans that turn your cash into savings, either through the medium of a company credit union or a bank, are an extremely useful means of sequestering money that might otherwise burn a hole in your pocket.

There are other ploys that can help you win the battle of the budget. If you've got a pay raise coming up, try to tuck all of it away. If you've paid off a loan, continue making the same payment to your bank account instead of letting it slip into the spending stream. Do the same at whatever point in the year Social Security deductions against your paycheck wind down. All of those suggestions are premised on the fact that you've been getting along somehow with less money, so why not put what is in effect a windfall to work for you?

Some windfalls you might just want to spend, and why not? A budget ought not to be graven in psychological stone. A budget is a roadmap and it ought to be flexible enough to change as the contours of your life and objectives change. It's the monitoring that counts. You want to know that you are using your money to get where you want to go. That means a modest amount of record keeping.

Keep your cash flow statement current and review it regularly, perhaps on a monthly basis, as a check on whether you've been able to make your budget cuts stick. Be flexible enough to make adjustments. Are your projections unrealistic? Are you squeezing too hard? Single-minded Micawberism might work out in a single person household, but if there are others around whose feelings have to be considered, watch out! There are more rewarding things to do than argue about money.

Most households these days are supported by "his" and "her" paychecks. It's absolutely essential to agree on who is going to pay for what. To some degree the agreement turns on stability of income. Maybe one of you is free lancing and can't count on any regular income. Maybe you're planning to start (or add to) a family, which is going to mean only one income for a while. In either of those cases, you might decide to budget as if there is only one income, and earmark whatever else comes in for savings or some other special purpose.

Some couples split their joint costs—rent, food, utilities and the like—right down the middle. Others split it proportionately, with the person who makes the least paying the least.

On a bookkeeping—and checking account—basis, there are three ways to handle things:

● You can pool both incomes and pay for everything out of the pool.

● Pool part of the incomes, keep the remainder separate.

● Keep both incomes separate, contribute individually to joint expenses.

There are pros and cons to each of those approaches. A complete pooling has the virtue of simplicity—one joint checking account, and a minimum of bookkeeping. The major potential stumbling block, as noted in a Bank of America consumer information study, "is the high degree of cooperation needed to keep a joint account in order."

The level of cooperation required involves more than just the mechanics of keeping the entries straight. That's a detail, although sometimes a confusing one. What's really at stake is the emotionally charged question of identity—who earned the money and where did it come from? The question has both psychological and legal overtones. In community property states such as California, some income is separate (dividends from a stock bought before marriage, for instance) and must be kept apart from such common income as salaries.

Option number two—pooling part of the income and keeping the rest separate—has the virtue of flexibility. There is no question about where the money needed for joint and individual purposes will come from. The cash is all nicely compartmentalized, but the compartmentalization means three checking accounts—two individual and one joint. And someone, of course, will have to agree to do the bookkeeping chores on the joint account.

Option number three—complete separation—preserves everybody's financial identity in a way that might be useful for business or tax reasons. On the other hand, the separatist approach can mean an awful lot of paper shuffling. The bills either get paid with two checks—one from each of the partners that add up to the total due—or one of you pays whatever is due and gets reimbursed by the other. Budgeting for two can be a fatiguing business, but it's better than not budgeting at all. That's as "true as turnips is . . . as true as taxes is," said Micawber, "and nothing's truer than them."

TOP DOLLAR TIPS

(1) Keep your cash flow chart up to date on a regular basis.

(2) Keep the stream of your cash flow from being

diverted by budgeting ahead for big ticket items—automobile insurance premiums, for example—that come up only once a year.

(3)   Keep your eyes peeled for budget leaks—a large number of checks written to cash, for example.

(4)   Paid off a loan? Continue making the payments, but this time to one of your reserve accounts instead of to the bank.

HOW TO MANAGE YOUR READY ASSETS

Chapter 2

More Interest on Your Savings

The meat packers have been making it big for years now by getting everything out of the pig except the squeal. That's not a bad money management precept, either. You want to get the highest return possible on your ready cash reserve, consistent with safety and liquidity—the ability to get at your money immediately whenever you need to.

Unless you're prepared to sleep on an excessively lumpy mattress, those requirements all add up to a bank of some kind or other—a commercial bank, a savings bank, a savings and loan assocaition, or a credit union. Safety first. Make sure you're dealing with an institution where your account will be covered up to the standard maximum of $40,000 by the Federal Deposit Insurance Corporation, or its equivalent.

After that, the big chore is to cut through all of the promotional hoopla and find out who is really paying the best return on the savings dollar. That isn't always easy. Often you have to fight yourself.

The mesmeric pull of such oft heavily advertised giveaways as hair dryers and digital clocks, citizens band radios and tennis racquets may blind you to the fact that you've tucked your nest egg into an institution that is offering less than the going rate. From the banker's point of view, it's a lot cheaper to pay for a truck load of "free" premiums than to tack another quarter-point interest on all the accounts in the shop.

Yet the "freebies" do have a way of enticing savers from one bank to another and not infrequently at some cost in interest. The ploy, though frowned on by regulatory authorities, works well enough for bankers to point with expansive pride to some branch offices they've built up with "the old pots and pans strategy." Underneath it all, most savers probably know there is no such thing as a free ride, but the allure of a giveaway is hard to fight.

So is the pull of convenience. In towns where there are competing banks, savers will often give up something in interest just because one institution may happen to be closer to the supermarket than another. In the cities, where there is almost always brisk competition for the saver's dollar, some people will literally not walk across the street to get a higher rate.

All of that is really short-sighted. There's more to

the search for higher rates than the psychological lift of having squeezed another quarter-point out of a banker who would much rather sell "friendly" service than a higher return to savers. Deposits, after all, are the banker's raw material and the imperatives of the business make him want to pay as little for that raw material as possible. The magic of compounding aside, rates do matter. It takes 16 years for money earning 4.5 percent to double. Money earning 5.5 percent doubles in 13 years.

Where are the best returns? By and large, they are in the so-called thrift institutions (savings banks and savings and loan associations), rather than in the commercial banks. In general, the thrift institutions are permitted to pay at least a quarter-percent more interest on savings than the commercial banks.

The difference, embodied in Federal law and the Federal Reserve Board's Regulation Q, reflects a difference in function. Commercial banks tend to concentrate on business loans, while thrift institutions tend to specialize in and are the nation's major source of residential mortgage loans. The rate spread is designed to encourage savers to tuck their money into the thrift institutions and thereby provide the steady flow of cash needed to keep the vital homebuilding industry hard at work.

Regulation Q has been changed in a number of respects since it was drafted back in the depression days of the 'thirties, ostensibly to curb what was regarded as ruinous rate competition between the commercial banks and the thrift institution.

Many commercial bankers argue that the regulation

should be scrapped entirely. There may well be changes in the wind. At the moment, however, the maximum allowable rate spread between the banks looks like this:

	Commercial Banks	Thrift Institutions
Regular Account	5%	5.25%
90-day	5.5%	5.75%
1 to 2½ years	6%	6.5%
2½ to 4 years	6.5%	6.75%
4 to 6 years	7.25%	7.5%
6 years or more*	7.5%	7.75%

*Most banks also offer special floating rate certificates on minimum deposits of $10,000 in maturities of six months or eight years. Interest payments are keyed to the discount rate on U.S. Treasury Bills.

The maximums, of course, are exactly that—a ceiling. There is no requirement that banks pay the maximum, and many do not. Thus, there are differences not only between classes of banks, but between banks within the same classification, as well. The shopper's search for truffles is often further complicated by differences in the kinds of accounts at the same bank. The differences reflect a constellation of factors—competitive pressures, branch locations, deposit mix, earning power, management strategy, and the condition of the money market.

The differences are sometimes very subtle, and can be detected only by shrewd comparative shopping. Take the example of the Dime Savings Bank of New York and the Brooklyn Savings Bank. At one point recently both New York City banks were paying the ceiling rate. Brooklyn Savings, however, was insisting on a $1,000 initial minimum deposit on all but its regular savings accounts. In other words, to get the best return on time accounts of one year or more you had to have a thousand dollars in hand.

The Dime Savings Bank, on the other hand, was taking $500 minimums on its 6.5 percent and 6.75 percent accounts and demanding the $1,000 minimum on only its 7.5 percent and 7.75 percent accounts. On the other hand, the depositor had to agree to keep his money at the Dime for at least 14 months to get 6.5 percent, while the term for the same rate at Brooklyn Savings was only one year. Your choice, of course, would depend on how much money you had to put away. In general, though, your strategy would be to stick with shorter maturities in a period of rising interest rates; longer ones in a period of declining rates.

One more illustration of how comparison shopping can help you get the best return on your savings dollar. The Citibank, like many commercial banks, was recently paying a sub-minimum 4.5 percent on its regular accounts. Depositors willing to sign up for a "statement savings" account, however, received the full 5 percent maximum. "Statement account" depositors got no passbook. They instead got a receipt for each of their transactions, and a full statement at the end of each quarter. Because Citibank was able to process statement accounts more cheaply than the traditional passbook variety, it was willing to go up another half point in interest on them.

Which account did depositors prefer? The lower paying regular passbook account, of course. Why?

"Apparently because they felt more secure having a passbook to hold and look at," notes an officer of the bank. Who says that psychology and saving don't mix and often to the detriment of the untutored depositor?

Even at the 5 percent maximum allowed commercial banks on regular savings accounts, the Citibank was paying less than its competitors. Interest on the accounts was compounded quarterly, while many other banks, both in New York City and elsewhere around the country, compound interest on a daily basis. The way in which interest is compounded and credited makes a significant difference. Daily compounding means that the interest on an account is computed each day, thereby adding bit by bit to the base on which the interest is calculated.

Thus, a basic 5.25 percent annual rate compounded daily works out to an effective rate of 5.47 percent a year; 6.5 percent compounded daily works out to an effective annual rate of 6.81 percent; and so on up the line to where the 7.75 percent maximum on term accounts of six years or more averages out to an effective rate of 8.17 percent.

Here's the check list. First, ask whether the bank is paying the maximum allowable rate. Establish whether the rate is being compounded on a daily basis, and then raise two other questions: how does the bank compute interest, and what types of accounts does it have available?

The best deal for the saver is the day-of-deposit to day-of-withdrawal crediting method. Interest is computed daily on however much money is in the account. Many banks, though, use one of three other methods—"low balance" (interest paid on the lowest amount of money in the account during the crediting period); first-in, first-out (withdrawals deducted from the starting balance); or last-in, first out (withdrawals deducted from the most recent deposits).

Studies done by Consumers Union and Professor Richard L.D. Morse, head of Kansas State University's Family Economics Department, have shown that the four different methods, applied to four identical accounts over the same three-month period, resulted in interest payments that ranged from $44.93 (low balance approach) to $75.30 (day-of-deposit-to-withdrawal). Another clear-cut demonstration of why it pays to read the fine print and ask questions. As Consumers Union has noted, the "frequency of crediting and compounding should be identical to be meaningful." Some banks, for example, will advertise daily compounding, but credit on only a quarterly basis. That means your money doesn't get the full effect of the compounding unless it's been on deposit for the entire quarter.

The way interest is credited and compounded is particularly important for systematic savers—individuals who bank a specific amount each month and who rarely make withdrawals.

Savers of that kind, says Bernard McDermott, a vice-president of the Dime Savings Bank, are probably better off in a regular than in a day-of-deposit to day-of-withdrawl type account. DW's are best for in-and-out savers whose thrift account tends to look like a checking account in slow motion. DW accounts do not reward systematic savers with the "grace days" many banks offer only on regular accounts. A saver who makes a deposit within the grace period—often the first 10 days of the month—is entitled to the same amount of interest as if the money had gone into the account on the first day of the month. The effect is a 10-day bonus that could amount to as much as 120 extra days interest a year for savers who budget their deposits on a monthly basis.

For many, budgeting savings on a regular basis may be even more important than the kind of account the money goes in. Discipline is a hardbought thing. That's one of the reasons why payroll deduction plans can be extremely useful. The money comes right off the top in what is essentially a forced form of saving.

The checkoff works particularly well with credit unions—the 20,000 or so affinity groups formed as co-operatively owned banks. Most such groups are by-products of business organizations, but the definition of affinity has been very liberally construed by both state and federal regulatory authorities. Thus, the Boston Symphony has a credit union and so does the Lee family—the Chinatown Lees, that is, and not the famous Virginia variety. There is even a credit union made up of Arabian horse breeders.

Credit unions are big business. Some 35 million Americans—one out of every six—have their savings stashed away in credit unions, partly because of the convenience of payroll deduction savings. There is another attraction. Many credit unions pay higher rates than other thrift institutions, although the same compounding and crediting caveats apply to them as to any other savings outlet.

Because credit unions are co-ops, their operating expenses tend to be quite low, a characteristic that has a decidely beneficial effect on the money they are able to pay out to members. At last report, 55 percent of all federally chartered credit unions were paying more than 6 percent a year. About 14 percent were paying between 6 and 7 percent, and 11 percent were paying 7 percent or more.

Federally chartered credit unions were recently given a big leg up when Congress permitted them to start offering certificates of deposit paying a maximum interest rate of 7.75 percent—the same maximum allowed other thrift institutions.

There is a big difference, though. In order to get that rate at a savings bank or a savings and loan association, you have to agree to leave your money on deposit for six years or more. Any money withdrawn before that time, as with all such time deposits, is subject to very stiff interest forfeiture penalties. The Congress, however, did not impose any such time requirements on the credit unions. Thus, a few have begun to offer the maximum 7.75 percent for cash left on deposit for as little as one year.

That is quite an attraction and depends, notes Lawrence Connell Jr., head of the National Credit Union Administration, "on a particular credit union and its earning power." "Many savers," continues the man who regulates the nation's 13,000 federally chartered credit unions, "can do better at credit unions than at savings banks or savings and loan associations, but they must shop and compare to know what they are getting."

Much the same observation applies to U.S. savings bonds. They, too, can be bought through payroll deduction and thus carry the same appeal as any other forced form of saving. The big question, though, is whether the bonds are really competitive with and have as much to offer as other forms of saving.

Here's how they work.

The ever popular series E bond is sold in minimum denominations of $18.75 and matures in five years to $25—until the end of 1979, that is. The Treasury, in a fit of revisionism aimed at reducing paper work, has decided to phase out the durable old E bond in favor of the new-fangled EE bond. The old $18.75 bond, beginning with the New Year 1980, becomes an official victim of inflation. The new minimum purchase price goes to $25 and will buy a face value which matures at $50 after eleven years and nine months. Other denominations range from $75 and $100 on up to maximums of $5,000 and $10,000. Series H bonds are sold in minimum denominations of $500 and mature in 10 years. The interest on the H bonds is paid semi-annually. Not so the E (or EE) bonds, which are sold on a "discount" basis. The interest payment on them is built into the difference between the price at which they are bought and the price at which they mature.

Both types of bonds must be held to maturity to return the full 6 percent interest they promise, but that will also change with the advent of the new HH bond. Unlike the old H bonds still slogging their way to maturity, the new HH will carry a straight 6 percent rate from the day of purchase—a modest bit of sweetener to help drum up sales. The old bonds can be cashed in at any time, but there are heavy incentives to hang on to them. In the first year of its life, the yield on an E bond is only 4.54 percent—far less than can be got in most thrift institutions. At the end of two years, the yield rises to 4.76 percent. It climbs bit by bit to 13 percent in the last six months of the five-year term to produce an average return to 6 percent. The same pattern holds for EE bonds.

There is nothing particularly exciting about that return, but it has to be balanced against some modest tax advantages. Like all Government securities, E and H bonds are exempt from state and local taxes. Further, the Federal tax on E bonds is not due until they are redeemed, and the maturity keeps getting extended. The extension amounts to as much as 15 years in the case of all E bonds bought since the end of 1973. Earlier dated maturities (those sold between May 1941 and April 1952, for instance) were stretched out for 40 years.

The deferral feature has made savings bonds a useful way of building up a tax-sheltered college education or retirement fund. Many forward-looking families begin accumulating E bonds in their children's names very early on. Some of the accumulation, in fact, starts with Baptism or Bar Mitzvah gifts. "They're great for Bar Mitzvahs and birthdays," says Sally Heinemann, a money market specialist for *The New York Times*. "They cost you only $18.75 and everybody gives you credit for spending $25."

When the college years begin and the bursar's office starts digging deep into everybody's pocket, the student dips into the hoard of E bonds. As long as the interest on the bonds, plus all of the student's other unearned income is less than $750, the ride is tax-free. And even if the deal isn't totally tax-free, the student is usually in a low enough income bracket so that the Internal Revenue Service bite won't hurt all that much.

The strategy is basically the same with building a retirement fund—take advantage of the tax deferral during your comparatively high income working years, cash the bonds in during the comparatively low income retirement years. Many retirees, in fact, stretch out the deferral by "rolling over" their E bonds into the longer maturity H bonds. The roll over is a tax-free event, and it is a way of converting the capital that has accumulated in the E bonds into a steady 6 percent return paid semi-annually. There are, of course, equally safe and better returns to be found elsewhere.

Thus, depending on how much of a premium you place on the convenience of forced payroll savings, E and H bonds really don't hold up on a yield basis with thrift institution term accounts. That doesn't mean, of course, that high yielding term accounts are the answer to all your saving needs. Because of the heavy penalties banks put on early withdrawals from term accounts, they definitely are not the repository for your rainy day, ready reserve emergency fund. If the car needs a ring job, or the dentist is bugging you for payment on all that root canal work, you want to be able to lay your hands on money you can use without taking a beating.

So, term accounts are a second line of defense—or offense. As such they have to compete on a yield basis with other safe, high return forms of investment that often have much more to offer in terms of liquidity. What we're talking about here are United States Treasury bills, notes, and Federal agency securities. There have been long periods when those so-called money market instruments have been a better deal than thrift institution time accounts.

One of those periods was during the great money crunches of the seventies when Treasury bills, regarded by the professionals as the nearest thing to cash, were yielding 8 percent or more. Deposits poured out of the banks in hot pursuit of those yields. Equally, of course, there have been times when safety and yield-oriented savers found they could do better at the banks. It all depends on what is happening in the money markets, and what the Federal Reserve Board is doing to fight inflation. You don't have to grope your way through the foggy recollections of Economics 108 to find out what's happening to interest rates. Check out *The Wall Street Journal*, or the financial pages of almost any serious daily and you should be able to find the "bill rate" without difficulty.

The bill rate is jargon for the yield on Treasury bills—short term Government I.O.U.s of three months, six months, or one year's duration. Because the bill rate varies with the gravitational pull of monetary policy, it is difficult to generalize on the generosity of the return you can expect on any given date of purchase. From the end of 1967 through 1978, however, there were only three years when the yield on 90-day Treasury bills fell below the maximum 5.25 percent allowable on regular thrift institution accounts.

Direct obligations of the U.S. Government, Treasury bills are as safe (maybe safer) as money in the bank, and if held to maturity carry no market risk at all. The bills are sold at weekly and monthly auctions. They can be bought directly through a regional Federal Reserve Bank at no cost, or through a local commercial bank at a charge of around $25.

The return on Treasury bills is liable to Federal taxes, but exempt from state and local levies—an important consideration in such high tax jurisdictions as New York, Massachusetts and Pennsylvania. There is one problem. Treasury bills are sold in minimum initial denominations of $10,000 and in multiples of $5,000 thereafter. Thus, for many savers they are out of reach. All of the regional Federal Reserve Banks provide sales information via special telephone lines and will supply a free copy of the informative "Basic Information on Treasury Bills" on request. For the location of the nearest Federal Reserve Bank, check with your own banker.

Treasury notes (they carry maturities of one to 10 years) and Treasury bonds (maturities of 10 years and up) are also worth taking a look at. Both the notes and the bonds are available in $1,000 and $5,000 denominations and they, too, often yield more than bank time deposits of comparable duration.

The same can be said of a rich alphabet soup of Federal agency securities, such as those issued by the

Banks for Cooperatives or the Federal Home Loan Banks. Some of the agency securities carry the full backing of the U.S. Government, others only an implied guarantee. All of them rank in the broadest band of the safety spectrum, however, and in general offer somewhat higher yields than direct Treasury obligations.

Two major agencies—the Bank for Co-Ops and the Federal Intermediate Credit Banks—usually come to market monthly with maturities of six and nine months, respectively. They are sold in denominations of $5,000 and up and help to finance the activities of the Farm Credit system, which provides loans to farmers, ranchers and their co-operatives.

Like Treasury obligations, all agency securities are exempt from state and local, but not Federal taxes and can be ordered through local commercial banks and some brokerage firms at a cost of about $25 per transaction. Information on upcoming sales can be found in newspaper financial pages, or in such services as Moody's Bond Survey or Standard & Poor's Fixed Income Investor. Many public libraries subscribe to one or both services, and so do the research departments of most brokerage firms.

A word of advice. Many commercial bankers, particularly in small towns, are sometimes not so well informed on agency securities as they might be. In the market for some Federal Land Bank bonds not long ago, I had to persuade the president of a fair-sized bank in suburban New Jersey (a) that the securities existed; (b) that they came in minimum denominations of $1,000; and (c) that they could *not* be bought from the Federal Reserve Bank. And he, nice gentleman, charged me only the standard $25 transaction fee for my expertise. Moral: if you put in an order for agency securities, do it in person rather than by telephone, and bring along either a newspaper clipping or a photocopy of one of the rating service reports so there won't be any mistakes about what you want to buy.

There are other money market instruments to think about—bank certificates of deposit and bankers' acceptances, for example. They are all higher yielding than regular savings accounts. Savings certificates keyed to the Treasury bill rates are available only in initial minimum denominations of $10,000. In larger denominations they tend to be institutional rather than individual investment vehicles. Commercial paper—short term corporate I.O.U.s—sold directly to investors by such blue chip corporations as General Motors Acceptance Corp. is another high-yielding possibility worth taking a look at.

Even blue chip commercial paper is not without some risk, but risk and higher rewards go hand in hand. G.M.A.C. paper ranges in maturity from one to 270 days and, depending on the doings of the money market, will generally offer yields of more than a point over the comparable bank rate. For more information on G.M.A.C. commercial paper, write the company's headquarters at 767 Fifth Avenue, New York 10022, or any of its 11 regional offices in such major cities as Atlanta, Boston and Chicago.

If you prefer not to dabble in the money market on

your own, you might consider buying the shares—
and professional management—of one of the 50 or so
money management mutual funds that have sprung
up over the last couple of years.

Among the biggest funds in the field are Dreyfus
Liquid Assets and Merrill Lynch Ready Assets, run by
such familiar names as the Dreyfus Corp. of the old
Wall Street lion fame and the thundering herd of
Merrill Lynch, Pierce, Fenner & Smith.

Sales of the funds have all but torn through the roof,
partly because sophisticated savers have begun to
realize that the investment companies offer a comparatively safe high yielding alternative to the thrift
institutions, particularly during periods of rising
short term interest rates.

All of the funds are "open-end," which is to say
they continuously sell shares in themselves and stand
ready to redeem shares whenever an investor wants to
cash them in. A few of the funds tack a sales charge on
share purchases, most do not. Most charge management fees of ½ of 1 percent of assets and most have the
same basic objective—to provide maximum current
income with minimum capital risk.

As the name suggests, the funds invest in a variety
of money market instruments. Some concentrate exclusively on Treasury bills and other government securities. Others vary the mix with certificates of deposit and commercial paper. Some like to keep the
maturities of the securities they buy short—as short,
in some cases, as an average of seven days. Funds
with short average maturities and a high concentra-

tion of "Governments" are generally less risky than those with a long average maturity and a high concentration of, say, commercial paper. On the other hand, to generalize again, higher risk means higher yield.

How safe are the money market funds? Pretty safe, but they are not banks. They do not offer the safety net of deposit insurance if something goes sour, and because they are subject to the play of the market, the money market funds cannot guarantee a stated return for any given period as the banks do.

What the money market funds do have to offer, of course, is diversification—investment in a broad spread of instruments that in itself provides a form of safety. Some funds require fairly high minimum initial purchases of $5,000. Others will settle for $1,000 or less for openers. Thus, many of the funds enable investors to buy into a package of securities they might not otherwise be able to afford—an equity in a packet of Treasury bills, for example, which can be bought directly only in denominations of $10,000 or more.

The combination of diversity, high yield, and liquidity—no penalties for cashing in shares that will be redeemed at any time—has given the money market funds a strong selling point against the banks. The funds credit dividends daily and most offer checking services that have become a strong sales point, too. The money market funds are in effect interest bearing checking accounts.

For more information on the funds, their investment policies and performance, consult the Wiesenberger Investment Companies Service, or Donoghue's

Money Fund Report, Box 542, Holliston, Mass. 01746. Both the Wiesenberger directory and the Donoghue Report, published weekly, can be found in many libraries and brokerage firms.

TOP DOLLAR TIPS

(1)   Shop the banks for the best return on savings accounts you can find. Savings banks and savings and loan associations usually pay higher rates than commercial banks.

(2)   Day-of-deposit to day-of-withdrawal accounts pay best for those whose savings accounts look like a checking account in slow motion.

(3)   A credit union may be the best place to keep a long term time deposit. Many, unlike other thrift organizations, charge no penalty on cash withdrawn before the account matures.

(4)   U.S. Savings Bonds bought through payroll deductions are a convenient way to forced saving, but in themselves, not a best buy.

Chapter 3

Better Checking Accounts

If there is one thing the *midinettes* in the promotional *ateliers* of the banks do best, it is embroidery. Think of the advertising alley dazzle that suffuses the plain old checking account. There are NOW accounts, "Good Deal Checking," "Custom Plans" and hundreds of other permutations, all designed to persuade customers that they are getting the best possible package. The best possible package is one in which you are (a) charged nothing at all for the service; and (b) get some interest return on your money.

Many banks advertise "free" checking—no service charges, no administrative charges, no charge at all except $2 or $3 per hundred or so for the checks themselves. Still others will advertise "free" checking that is free only if you agree to keep a minimum balance in the checking account itself, or in a savings account that may or may not be generating the maximum allowable rate of interest. That's not really free checking, although the interest offset helps.

The banks—and their quite powerful lobbies—have been arguing about the virtues of paying interest on checking account deposits for years now. The argument is a relic of the 'thirties. The condition of many commercial banks was so parlous that interest payments on checking account deposits were outlawed.

Some maverick bankers, revisionist historians all, argue that the ban was unnecessary, and just one more example of pussy-footed regulators acting on behalf of the regulated instead of the consumer. It was an argument that took a long time to bear fruit. Not until 1973 was the Congress persuaded that there were competitive merits to permitting thrift institutions to pay interest on checking accounts. The approach was gradualist. The privilege was tendered first only to thrifts in Massachusetts and New Hampshire, then extended to the whole of New England on a trial basis.

The consumer response was interesting. The so-called NOW accounts (for negotiable order of withdrawal) expanded rapidly. Some of the demand came from alert consumers outside of New England who learned that they could finesse the regulatory *cordon sanitaire* imposed on the rest of the country by opening NOW accounts by mail. The First National Bank of Boston, for example, at last report had more than 40,000 NOW accounts on its books. About 5,000 of those originated from outside the New England area, including what the bank said was "every state in the union," as well as some depositors in "Europe and the Mid-East."

The response from out-of-staters was good for several reasons. Banking by mail is clearly less convenient than walking down the block to a local branch office, but no great hardship. There was little difficulty in getting out-of-state checks honored, and there were definite advantages to both the interest payments and the slower time in which the checks cleared.

Though there was no great stampede to the New England NOW accounts, the movement was significant enough for the commercial banks to get their competitive guard up. After a lot of wrangling, Congress gave commercial banks everywhere the right to offer NOW accounts, too. The commercial bankers stole a march on their arch rivals, the savings institutions, by persuading the legislators to eliminate the ¼ point higher rate the thrifts were permitted to pay on their version of the interest-bearing checking account.

There are advantages to interest-bearing checking accounts, of course, but they may not be as marked as the advertising suggests. In fact, for many there might be an outright disadvantage in going to a NOW account. It all depends on the size of the minimum balances you are required to keep on tap, the number of checks you write a month, and the bank's fee structure.

The mix varies, but the package being pushed by one major New York City commercial bank is not atypical. In effect, the package has two parts—a checking account and a savings account that pays 5 percent, compounded quarterly. As checks are presented for payment, the computers automatically switch cash from the savings account to the checking account. Thus, the interest clock is running all the time.

The cost? A monthly fee of $5 on balances of less than $1,000. That works out to $60 a year—much more than would be earned in interest on $1,000 left on deposit for a year in a regular savings account. The fee scales downwards on accounts of more than $1,000 and drops to zero on balances of $5,000 or more. By way of comparison, the same bank—and many of its competitors—has long offered absolutely free checking to depositors who keep $500 on tap in either a checking or a savings account.

As always, it pays to read the fine print. NOW accounts offer real leverage only to those who carry fairly high balances and write comparatively few checks. Conversely, individuals who keep their balances low and write a lot of checks are better off exploring other alternatives.

The alternatives are plentiful. Among the most intriguing options are the checking account services provided by most money market mutual funds. They are for the most part truly free. Only a few of the funds charge extra for checks drawn against share accounts. Most cover the cost of the service out of their overall management fee.

There are two major advantages to money market fund checking. One of them is that the money behind the check—the fund shares, really—continues to draw daily interest until the check is presented for payment to the fund's bank. On average that can mean as much as a week or more of additional interest. Further, the funds work hard at maximizing the so-called float—the time it takes a check to clear—by taking advantage of geography and the snail-like rhythms of the U.S. Postal Service.

Many professional money managers do the same thing. Many corporations and brokerage firms, for example, stretch out the demands on their own cash flow by paying East Coast suppliers or customers through a West Coast bank, West Coast customers through an East Coast bank. The ploy slows the collection process and reduces the amount of temporary borrowing that has to be done to keep working capital levels up to snuff.

If your favorite broker is working that gambit with you, thereby putting you in a position where your own bank might not let you draw on an out-of-state check for a week or so, tell him to knock it off. Insist on being paid through a bank in your own Federal Reserve region.

On the other hand, there is no good reason why you shouldn't force your creditors to play with the sun in their eyes if you can get away with it. You've got a cash position to protect, too, and there's no reason why you shouldn't try to squeeze as much advantage out of the postal float as everyone else.

The Capital Preservation Fund, Inc., of Palto Alto,

Calif., for example, has given its shareholders a lift by setting up a network of four different clearing banks located in Great Falls, Mont., San Francisco, Miami and Providence, R.I. The spread between those locations has a marked effect on the payment cycle—and the longer the cycle, the better the return on your money.

There is one problem. The checking service is a useful sales tool, but the funds see themselves first and foremost as money managers rather than clearing house advisers. Thus, most of them limit the size of the check that can be written against an account to a minimum of $500. Some, on the other hand—Federated Money Market, Inc., 421 Seventh Ave., Pittsburgh, Pa. 15219, for example—have cut the minimum to $250.

The minimum may be too big for some, but many market fund shareholders have found it useful to pay regular monthly bills out of a single large check deposited in their regular commercial bank accounts just before the bills are paid. The New York Times "Market Place" columnist Robert Metz, for example, discovered one Capital Preservation Fund shareholder who lives in Miami and pays his $1,000 a month rent through the money manager's California clearing bank. Thanks to the additional float time, he picks up an extra five days interest on the $1,000 twelve times a year.

Money market fund checks are particularly useful if you've got to put cash in escrow—the down payment on a house for example, where you might have to wait a couple of weeks before title to the dwelling changes hands. The frosting on the cake is even richer if you're dealing with payees that are slow in bundling payments off to the bank.

One major offender (or deserving victim) is the United States Government at tax time. The I.R.S. is overwhelmed with uncashed checks and often underwhelmed by the temporary help it takes on to deal with the April 15th Saturnalia. Capital Preservation likes to talk about the wealthy West Coast shareholder who paid a $176,000 tax bill on April 15 with a check drawn against a New England bank. The check did not clear until May 1, thereby giving the investor an additional $600 interest on his account. Many colleges, despite the financial ills endemic in academe, are also notoriously slow in cashing tuition checks.

Playing the checking and postal float is a little like playing musical chairs. Somewhere along the line there has to be a fall guy. It is a game that bankers do not like to play unless things go their way. Policies vary from bank to bank, and even from customer to customer. A senior editor of the Foreign Policy Association in New York City, for example, is regularly allowed to draw immediately against out-of-town checks at a branch of the Marine Midland because she has been banking there for years and has a fairly sizable account. Other less well known customers might have to wait as long as five business days for an out-of-town check to clear before being allowed to draw against it. "We do things for good customers that have been with us for some time that we won't do for new accounts that have just walked in the door," says a Marine Midland officer. That generalization holds almost everywhere, and is a good business reason for finding a bank you like and sticking with it.

It is equally good business, however, to shop around and see what the policy is. Some banks like to play the float, too, and will hold up payment on a check longer than they need to. There are strong profit incentives for the banks to squeeze an extra day or two of free use out of depositors' cash. Doing so can either reduce their need to borrow, or provide them with money to lend other banks.

Sometimes there is just plain confusion on both sides of the bank counter about what the holding period is. Take the case of Matthew Bassity, a tough-minded editor who for years helped to put out the *International Herald Tribune* and who under the same eye shade mustered all of the tact and diplomatic skills it took to serve as president of the wildly idiosyncratic Overseas Press Club of America.

One soft April morning not long ago, Matt opened two accounts in the Greater New York Savings Bank with a check totaling $688.01. Some $300 went into a regular checking account and the balance into a savings account from which transfers could be made into the checking account by telephone. In the next month or so, there were two small withdrawals against the checking account—one for $20 and the other for $15.

Then there was a whacking big deposit that cheered Matt no end—a $2,052.16 refund check from the Internal Revenue Service. The essence of happiness is to share it and Matt did exactly that by writing a check for $400 to one of his sons. That was on May 27. A couple of days later Matt went down to the bank to draw a $900 check for his regular monthly alimony payment, and the administrative roof fell in. Matt was told flatly that the $400 check to his son had bounced. He was also told that he could not write the alimony check without it bouncing, too. The reason: the $2,000 I.R.S. check that more than covered both payments had not been in the account long enough to clear.

Matt Bassity did a slow burn. The I.R.S. check, he told an assistant vice-president, was "as good as cash." The bank officer was polite, but unmoved. There was a 30-day hold before out-of-town checks could be drawn on, he said, and the I.R.S. check was manifestly from out-of-town. As it turned out, the A.V.P. was wrong. The bank's policy on out-of-town checks was not 30 days, but 14 days. In the end, somewhat more sensible higher authority intervened and Matt was permitted to draw his alimony check, but only on the condition that he submit to a hold on the $628 in his savings account.

Atrocity stories like that are commonplace. Many bank employees are badly briefed. And customers are often unaware of the holding period on checks. They wind up in the same infuriating bounced check hassle as Matt Bassity because many banks just don't put the same effort into explaining the workings of the system as they do into hyping the superlatives of supposedly "free" checking.

There are good reasons for that. Many big city commercial banks have worked hard to cut the clearing time on local checks to two, maybe three days and on out-of-town checks to around seven days. That's good computerization. Many thrift institutions, however, do not handle their own clearing operations. They rely on commercial banks to do the job and that adds several days to the process. Bankers, of course, are not chained to the float. They're entitled to some discretion in deciding whether you can draw on a check—even if it is from out-of-town and is not entirely backed by a cash balance.

If you've got a problem, talk to a bank officer. If you've been a customer for a long time, lay heavy stress on your "banking relationship." If you don't like the answers you get, exercise your own discretion, and take your account elsewhere. You might be agreeably surprised with the change.

There is nothing agreeable about a check that bounces. They are almost invariably the result of misunderstanding, or miscalculation, and at penalty charges of $5 and up, can get awfully expensive. The best solution is to take a sharp pencil to your check book accounting because the protection against bounced checks offered by many banks—overdraft checking—is a fairly expensive proposition, too.

Overdraft checking, known around the country as "checking plus" and other such soothing names, is nothing more than a checking account backed by a line of credit. The credit picks up if a check bounces, typically at an annual rate of 12 percent, and, of course, can be used for other purposes as well.

If you're in the habit of bouncing a lot of checks, overdraft privileges might save you some money, but don't count on it. The 12 percent rate runs until everything is all paid up and the psychological pressure of having a line of credit is no different than having a credit card in your hot hand. Both beg to be used.

Checking accounts beg to be used, too, and how much use you make of one is probably the best guide to the kind of account you should choose. The best deal is unlimited checking at no charge, preferably in an interest-bearing account with no conditions attached—no minimum balances and no maintenance charges.

Most banks, however, key their charges to some combination of the number of checks you write or the size of the balances you keep on hand. If your balances are high and you write few checks, you might be able to do without a checking account entirely. Many thrift institutions will write third party checks against withdrawals at no charge, depending on the size of the check. The variations are endless. As always, the rule should be to air and compare. If you're dealing with an activity plan, zero in on the monthly maintenance fees and cost per transaction. If the bank is offering a minimum balance plan, check out how the balance is calculated and the service charge levied if you fall below the balance. How much do the checks themselves cost? How much do overdraft charges run and what does it cost to stop payment on a check?

All of that may seem like a lot to ask, but it's basic to the arithmetical work that will help you figure out which kind of account is best for you. In general, activity plans are the best bet for individuals who write comparatively few checks and keep low balances. The minimum balance plans are the best bet for individuals who write a lot of checks and can manage to keep their balances at a commensurately high level.

TOP DOLLAR TIPS

(1) The best checking account is one that carries absolutely no charges, and pays interest to boot.

(2) To squeeze the utmost out of the "float"—and get a good return on your balances as well—look into the money market mutual funds.

(3) Longtime customers with an established "banking relationship" may use their position to negotiate better checking privileges. If there's no give, take your money elsewhere.

(4) Stay away from overdraft checking accounts. They are not a free accommodation to keep your checks from bouncing. They are lines of credit that cost you 12 percent a year.

Chapter 4

Borrowing Money

Operating on borrowed money makes a lot of people edgy, but think of credit as being one more tool in your money management kit. Capital is so hard to accumulate that most of us find it far more sensible to go to the money lenders than to dip into assets to buy an automobile, a big ticket appliance, or even a college education. So long as you stay within sensible parameters, it's comparatively easy to budget installment payments, and there's satisfaction in knowing that you're taking in Uncle Sam as a partner. Interest payments are tax deductible.

The higher your tax bracket, the more the interest deductions are worth. In general, though, the search should be for the lowest possible cost. One of the best places to look is your life insurance policy. If you have taken on ordinary rather than term coverage, there are strong incentives for borrowing against the cash build-up on a pure investment basis.

In most states, it is still possible for most policy holders to borrow against life insurance at the very low rate of 5 percent a year. In some cases, if you pre-pay the interest, the effective rate can be cut to 4.8 percent. On dividend paying participating policies, the effective rate is even lower.

In general, depending on your family needs and overall financial situation, it is probably not a good idea to pump the proceeds of an insurance loan into a hot little $2 oil stock you think is going to go to $50 overnight. The whole idea of insurance is protection and most insurance loans get paid back only at the death of the policy holder out of the face amount of the coverage. The cost of liquidating the loan leaves just that much less for the beneficiaries. There is no such subtraction—in fact there is an addition—if the loan has been put into some safe, high yielding alternative form of investment—Treasury bonds, or investment grade corporates, for example.

It is a tack familiar to many sophisticated money managers—a way of turning a profit on a difference in yield spreads. The level of insurance loans, in fact, tends to move pretty much with the interest cycle. When money market rates hovered around their all-time high in the seventies, for example, cash value borrowings climbed to 8.7 percent of the industry's assets—the highest level since the Depression year of

1935. In that forlorn year, people were probably borrowing to cover such basic needs as food and rent, or because it was the only way they could manage to keep paying their premiums.

Lately though, the incentives have been of a different order. Cash borrowed at 5 percent could be plunked into a nice safe Government and Federal agency securities yielding around 9 percent or 10 percent. The incentives are still there. Even so conservative an option as long term savings certificates yield more than 8 percent a year on a daily compounding basis.

Are there any potential booby traps in borrowing against insurance cash values? For some people, perhaps, a loss of flexibility. Cash values can be converted into paid-up life insurance and that can be an attractive option for older people whose need for protection is no longer so large as when the family was growing up.

If you're going to manage your money, it seems to me you should always shoot for the highest yield you can get, consistent with safety. For years many insurance companies played straight to that dictum. The availability of cheap 5 percent money was part of the sales pitch. The asset drain that started with the great money crunch of '74, however—and rising interest rates generally—set the industry to thinking second thoughts. Thanks to a heavy and highly successful lobbying campaign, almost every state legislature in the country has given insurance companies the right to raise the loan rate from 5 percent to 8 percent a year. The right is permissive, not mandatory, and it applies only to policies written after the effective date of legislation that varies from state to state.

The higher rates in most cases cannot be levied on those who bought their coverage during the long honeymoon of 5 percent money. Some companies, because they see cheap loan rates as a useful selling point, have not gone to the full 8 percent.

Even 8 percent money is still a good buy, except for lower cost loans you might be able to swing at an ethnic or a fraternal organization. The 8 percent compares favorably with two other low cost options— bank passbook loans and loans collateralized by stock. Most banks and savings and loan associations will lend you up to 90 percent of what you have in a savings account at around a point above the interest rate on the account itself. Commercial banks will lend up to 70 percent of the market value of listed stocks at about a point over the "prime" rate—the rate charged the very best blue chip corporate credit risks. In both cases, you have to leave the collateral—passbook or stock certificate—in the hands of the bank. You can continue to make deposits (and withdrawals) above the amount of collateral the bank wants held in a savings account loan.

Nothing makes a banker feel more secure than highly liquid collateral, hence low rates whose effective costs are made even lower by the dividends you continue to collect on either the passbook or the securities. Practices vary from bank to bank, but in many cases you can continue to roll over the loan for an extended period so long as you keep your interest payments up to snuff. Many big brokerage firms are also accommodating about making low cost loans against securities. Merrill Lynch, Pierce, Fenner & Smith, for example, was among the first brokerage firms to take the traditional margin account loan and tie it to both a credit card and special checks. The combination for the first time enabled clients to tap free credit balances in a margin account directly without going through the time-consuming business of asking (and waiting for) the brokerage firm to issue a check.

The rates on most collateralized loans—insurance, passbook and securities—are invariably quoted on the "simple" interest basis you learned about way back there in the fifth grade. If you borrow $1,000 and the rate is 8 percent, you know your interest cost is going to be $80 a year.

The best credit of all, of course, is when you have the interest-free use of somebody else's money— department store or credit card purchases, for example, on which there are no interest charges if you pay your bill in full within the stipulated 25- to 30-day billing period. If you extend the payment, though, you get hit with a finance charge that amounts to between 12 percent and 18 percent a year.

Whether it's "open-end" (credit card and revolving charge accounts, for example, where you can vary the monthly payments) or "closed-end" (auto loans, for example, where the size of the monthly payments are fixed), borrowing can be a costly business. Rates vary from lender to lender, and it's impossible to shop intelligently without knowing something about the mechanics of the trade.

For openers, credit unions generally charge lower rates than commercial banks, and commercial banks are generally cheaper than finance companies. Finance companies charge more for their money because they are more likely to take on risks that other lenders will not.

Many lenders, at least for internal use, still talk in terms of "add on" rates. Let's say you want to borrow $1,000 for a year. The quoted rate is 6 percent, which on a simple interest basis would mean you'd be paying $60 for the use of the money. The lender, however, adds on the $60 with the result that you pay back $1,060 in 12 equal installments of $88.33 a month. Since you have the full use of the $1,000 only in the first month, and on a declining basis thereafter, your true interest cost is roughly twice the simple interest cost, or about 12 percent.

Installment loans also used to be quoted on a discount basis, under which you'd have to borrow roughly $1,064 to get the $1,000. The result is a slightly higher cost than with the add-on method, and an effective rate of 12 percent.

Both methods are shot through with such ambiguity as to make meaningful rate comparisons difficult. After a lot of tugging and hauling by consumer groups, Congress finally passed a Truth in Lending law that requires lenders to quote the effective rate only, the so-called APR or annual percentage rate. You'll see the term spelled out in boldface on most loan applications. The same law requires lenders to spell out the finance charge in dollars. The finance charge includes not only interest, but any other items—credit life insurance and service fees, for example—factored into the cost of the loan. Each of the costs must be detailed separately, and then totaled. When you compare rates, match up both the APR and the finance charge, and go where the best deal is. And the best deal need not include insurance that will pay off the loan if you die before it has been amortized. The principle stands. Insure against the big risks, let the little ones take care of themselves.

When you shop for credit, don't be afraid to bargain. If you've been dealing with a bank for some time, try to squeeze a bit out of your "banking relationship." Insert the term into the conservation like a nicely greased thermometer, and mention in passing the size of your checking and savings account balances. If that doesn't get you at least a centigrade or so more cordiality—to say nothing of a quarter to a half point lower rate—maybe it's time to consider taking your business to a more receptive environment. Keep screwed firmly in mind the premise that loan rates can be shopped, and that they are negotiable.

One other thing to keep in mind with department store or credit card revolving credit: The APR can be the same, but your total finance charge varies with the way your loan balance is computed. There are four different methods of doing so—adjusted balance, average adjusted daily balance, balance after deduction, and previous closing balance. Without going into the arcana of it all, the adjusted balance method is cheapest for the consumer, the balance after deduction and the average adjusted daily balance methods the most expensive.

Most banks—and bank credit cards—are keyed to the average adjusted daily balance method. Tinkering with the billing cycle, in fact, is one way lenders can maximize their returns without being too obvious about it. The Citibank, for example, not long ago ended the free ride for its Master Charge card holders by levying a minimum 50 cent finance charge on individuals who paid their bills within the 25-day grace period.

There was a howl from people who had taken out the Citibank card precisely because it was "free"— free in the sense of no charge on bills paid during the grace period, and free of up-front costs such as the $20 annual fee American Express and other travel and entertainment companies levy against their card holders.

Few other banks followed the Citibank lead, but some got much the same effect with a little fine tuning on the way outstanding loan balances were figured. Where there were loan balances outstanding, the interest clock started running at the moment the Master Charge computers received a bill instead of from the billing date itself.

Complexities of that kind are rife in the cashless society the big five credit card companies are trying to create. There are two threshold questions. Should you have a credit card at all? And if so, which one? The cards certainly offer convenience.

Travel and entertainment (T & E) cards such as American Express and Diners Club are an open sesame to most of the world's great restaurants and hotels, while the more retail-oriented Master Charge and Visa cards find ready entree in most stores of even modest pretension. Increasingly, both types of card companies are trying to penetrate each other's prime markets. More restaurant windows are bursting out in a fever of Master Charge and Visa decals, more stores are flying the blue and white of American Express. So there is convenience aplenty. You don't have to carry around a lot of cash, and if a bargain new summer suit or a pair of shoes catches your eye, a judicious application of plastic money will help you snap it up. Like everything else, though, convenience has its price.

With a piece of plastic burning a hole in your pocket, it is much more difficult to fight off impulse purchases—the fun of dinner out, the textures of Pucci and Gucci—that can become real budget wreckers. At the end of every billing cycle, there is the *douloureuse.* Cash on the barrel head with the T & E cards, extended credit at 12 percent to 18 percent with the bank cards. If you are self-disciplined enough to resist the siren song of the full life, maybe you can afford a credit card.

Which one? That depends on your needs. The $20 annual fee on the T & E cards puts some people off, but if you charge more than $118 a year at 18 percent on a bank card you'll be laying out the equivalent of $20 anyway. The $20 charge is a kind of Chinese Wall between the T & E and the bank cards. It's the price you pay for the supposedly "free" use of American Express or Diners Club money. The banks, from the very beginning, have heavily promoted the idea of "free cards," but their plastic is the thin edge of the wedge. Two out of every three Citibank card holders, for example, are carrying installment loans at rates which in New York amount to 18 percent on the first $700, and 12 percent on everything over that amount.

The basic appeal of the T & E cards is to the expense account aristocracy, business people for the most part. Convenience aside, billings on the cards generate the kind of record needed to support the legitimacy of entertainment deductions with the I.R.S. That, in fact, is the basis on which James Conway, president of the Ayco Corp., a financial counseling concern, urges his clients to carry both types of cards—a T & E card for business and a bank card for personal spending.

"If you keep all of your office spending on the T & E card and have your wife keep buying the kids shoes and things like that on the bank card," Mr. Conway says, "you'll never have any trouble convincing the I.R.S. that personal expenses are not creeping into your business expenses."

Almost anyone who is solvent can get a bank credit card. The T & E companies tend to be a bit more selective, and apply pretty much the same criteria that bank officers use with applications for conventional installment loans.

Most lenders measure credit worthiness with a scoring system that includes such considerations as:

● Past Performance. What your credit record has been, how much money you owe, and how often you've borrowed.

● Age. Since older people tend to have better credit records, the scoring system carries a kind of built-in bias against individuals in their early twenties, who often cannot get credit without a co-signer.

● Stability. How long you've lived in a neighborhood, whether you own a house or rent; and the general level of your assets are all grist to the lender's mill.

● Income. The kind of job you have, the amount you make, and whether you're paid on a salary or a commission basis are all taken into account.

● Expenses. Number of dependents and size of debt repayments in relation to income.

It's especially worthwhile to keep those test questions in mind if you're applying for credit for the first time ever; if you've moved and are applying for credit for the first time in a new town; or if you're a married woman applying for credit for the first time in your own name. Credit applications tend to be monosyllabic. If you think you're likely to run into problems, why not reinforce the application with a résumé highlighting some of the virtues that will make you more credit-worthy.

Most people get turned down for one or more of several reasons: too little time in a neighborhood or in a job, too much debt outstanding or too little income to handle it, or an uneven repayment history.

If you get turned down, make sure the lender explains why. That's required under the Equal Credit Opportunity Act. Further, if you've been turned down because of background supplied by a credit reporting agency, the lender has to give you the name and the address of the outfit that supplied the information.

The Fair Credit Reporting Act entitles you to free access to the information in your credit file if you make a written request for it within 30 days of being turned down.

The credit reporting agencies have no more claim on infallibility than anybody else. You are entitled to have incorrect information expunged from the file. In cases where there is some dispute over the accuracy of the information, you have the right to insert your own explanation in the file and the right to insist that it be included in all future reports.

Even if you've not been turned down for a loan on the basis of your credit history, it's not a bad idea to check out your file from time to time. Ask your banker for the name of the credit agency he does business with. All such agencies are required to acquaint you with the "nature and substance" of what is in your file. Some agencies will mail you a copy of your report in response to a written request that includes your full name, your spouse's name and Social Security numbers. The charge for such a routine request typically runs to around $4 or $5. You can also make an appointment to drop by the agency and discuss the report in person.

A knowledge of the importance of the reporting agency's role is a must for married women who want to establish a credit identity of their own. Many such women are listed in the files under their husband's name. Under the Equal Credit Opportunity Act, women applying for a loan can insist that creditors take into consideration the history on any joint account.

Here, as detailed by the Federal Reserve Board, are some other highlights of the Equal Credit Opportunity Act:

● You can't be refused credit just because you're a woman, or just because you're married, single, separated, divorced or widowed.

● You can't be refused credit because you're of child-bearing age and a lender thinks your earning power might be cut by pregnancy.

● If you're relying on your income to carry a loan, information about your spouse or his cosignature can be required only under very limited circumstances.

In essence, what the law does is try to ensure that women are judged by the same loan standards as men. That doesn't mean, of course, that women are any more immune than men to the clamor of our consumer society. There are credit-holics of both sexes who want it all—and right now.

If 20 percent or more of your take-home pay is going for debt repayment, you know you've got trouble. There are some other early warning signals that you may be in over your head. Are you using cash advances on credit cards to meet such routine expenses as rent, mortgage payments or utility bills? Are you using new loans to pay off old ones, or in the market for a "consolidation" loan that will get all of your creditors under one roof?

If you do get into trouble, don't wait for your creditors to come to you. Go to them and try to work out a plan. Maybe you can persuade them to accept only interest payments, and hold off on the principal for a while. Maybe you can stretch out the terms of the loan. In some cases, you may not find any give on the banker's side at all, but it's better to make the effort than to let the default machinery take over automatically.

There is professional help to be had for the asking in most cities from non-profit Consumer Credit Counseling Services. The CCC's are experts at tailoring repayment schedules that both sides can live with. Financial and budgeting advice is their stock in trade, but there are times when intervention and counseling may not be enough.

Is personal bankruptcy a solution? Plenty of Americans apparently think so. The rising curve of inflation has made it harder than ever for people to keep up with the debt load. Many activist lawyers, in fact, argue that the Federal bankruptcy laws are a form of consumer protection. They are also a last resort, to be considered, says Legal Aid Society attorney Mort Dicker, only "when you can't pay your debts as they arise, no matter how much belt-tightening you do. When you can't lead a normal life, feed and shelter your family and at the same time meet your creditors' demands."

A new breed of lawyers like Mr. Dicker has helped to remove some of the stigma that personal bankruptcy used to carry. People are much more aware that bankruptcy is often as much the result of hard luck (a job loss) and emotional problems (alcoholism or a broken marriage) as bad management.

Something like 200,000 people a year wind up in

Federal bankruptcy court. Most are "no asset" cases, who emerge expunged of all debt except for such continuing obligations as alimony, child support, and some taxes. A minority of petitioners opt for Chapter XIII "wage earner" settlements under which the interest clock gets killed and creditors get repaid at least a portion of what they are owed over a long period of time.

There are do-it-yourself bankruptcy kits, but they require a lot of attention to detail. Standard legal fees run around $250 to $350 for individuals, not including the $50 filing fee, and in the $500 range for couples. Maybe the Legal Aid Society or some other public interest organization can help.

In some cases—if you work for a bank, a finance company or a collection agency, for example—bankruptcy may cost you your job. It also hangs like a miasma over your credit record for 14 years, but a trip through the courts is not the end of the credit line. With some effort, it may take no more than a couple of years to rehabilitate your standing. In fact, you may even find some lenders so eager to do business—at rates just this side of usury, of course—that they'll be waiting on the courthouse steps for you. This time they know they've really got you because you're not allowed to file for bankruptcy again for six long years.

TOP DOLLAR TIPS

(1) If you can borrow against your life insurance at low rates, why not invest the money elsewhere at higher rates?

(2) After insurance loans, the next cheapest way to borrow is against a savings account passbook or stock.

(3) Use "interest free" loans—department store or credit card charge accounts—but keep them free by paying off within the 25- to 30-day billing cycle.

(4) Do you really need the extra life or disability insurance the lender will try to sell when you borrow money? All it does is add to the cost of the loan.

Chapter 5

Meeting
College Costs

Back in the 'sixties, when the campuses were explosive with student unrest, I got a chuckle out of an overwrought neighbor. "Don't worry, Tim," she told one of my sons. "By the time you get ready to go to college, they'll all be burned down." Well, the colleges are there, and so is Tim. I am not chuckling. The worry is no longer "burn, baby, burn," but "bankruptcy, baby, bankruptcy."

Even the barest recital of the numbers evokes the spectre of bankruptcy. According to the Bowery Savings Bank, it cost the class of '48 at Harvard, Duke or Northwestern, a little under the grand total of $3,500 to get through four years of school. By 1955, the figure had jumped to $5,487. It is currently hovering around a tumescent $27,200, and no relief in sight. The going rate at many heavily subsidized state colleges is about $3,000 a year. That same college, assuming a modest inflation rate of only 6 percent a year, will be charging $35,520 a year when your one-year-old is ready to register for Economics 108.

The cost of a college education has far outstripped the rise in disposable income, and added oxygen to the flame of what has suddenly become a burning question: Is four years of advanced schooling really worth the expense involved? The manic swings of job openings—now not enough, now too many teachers and engineers—has left many young people totally disillusioned with the conventional wisdom that college is an automatic passport to the good life.

Education, of course, means a good deal more than a dollar and cents leg up the career ladder. Who can put a value on the business of becoming a person? The financial pressures are such, though, that it more than ever pays to get a good fix—and an early one—on how you're going to handle the bursar's bills. Two years before a student hopes to matriculate is not too soon to begin canvassing the possibilities. Waiting until half of senior year high school has whizzed by may be too late. Start by shedding some illusions. If you're in the $20,000 a year and up income bracket, don't count on anything more than token scholarship help, even if your child is very brainy. You might do better if your child is an exceptional athlete (the scouts are particularly hungry for good women athletes), but there is one thing you will have to reconcile yourself to.

If you are in what is vaguely delineated as the middle class, the colleges are going to insist you put up far more money than you ever thought you'd have to. The political weight of that reality has registered in Congress. The range of loan subsidies has gotten better, but not so much better that you won't feel the pinch. Take a family of four, with two children in college, a gross adjusted income of $27,000 and assets of $40,000. That's a not uncommon financial configuration in these inflated days of two paychecks when even the most modest home is likely to have a market value of close to $50,000. And when the financial aid people talk assets, they mean not only such liquid items as stocks, bonds and cash, but your equity in the old homestead as well. But there you are—going broke on $27,000 a year and your only asset to speak of is a house worth $40,000. Guess what your "expected contribution" for each of those two children is. It is exactly $2,875 each. A total of $5,750 after-tax dollars, that is.

The size of the expected family contribution is measured by an arcane but more or less standard formula applied to the Financial Aid Form or Family Financial Statement you file with either the College Scholarship Service (CSS), or the American College Testing Company (ACT). Different colleges use one or another of those corporations as clearing houses for both scholastic aptitude tests and the raw material on which estimates of financial need are based.

The family contribution really breaks down into two different income streams—the parents' and the student's. The former is based on net income and assets after certain allowances are made for income taxes, other expenses and family size. Among the expenses not taken into consideration are items that loom large in many budgets—tuition for children in private secondary schools, commuting costs, payments on an automobile, mortgage payments, and routine home repairs, for example. What's left over after the allowances have been skimmed off the top is multiplied by a "taxation rate." That determines the magic number—the parents' contribution.

The student's contribution is based on 35 percent of savings or any other assets, plus an assumption of $400 worth of pre-freshman year summer earnings. Put it all together, and you've got the family contribution. So there won't be any surprises—or damaged illusions—write for a free booklet, "Meeting College Costs," put out by the College Entrance Examination Board. Write College Board Publications Orders, Box 2815, Princeton, N.J. 08540. Using the worksheets in the booklet will give you a good idea of where you stand.

The next element to take up is the cost of going to college—tuition and fees, room and board, transportation, books, and such personal expenses as clothing, laundry, and recreation. Some of those costs are pretty much the same everywhere. Unless a student lives at home, board and personal expenses won't vary much no matter what the school. Tuition is the real killer. It might range from $500 a year at a state university to $4,500 a year and up at some prestigious private college. Transportation costs, of course, are a function of distance.

Try the numbers in a couple of different ways—living at a state university or a private college; commuting to either; maybe doing the first two years of undergraduate study at a low-cost community college. You can get a good rundown on comparative costs from *The College Handbook,* available at most libraries, and you certainly want to study the catalogues of the colleges that seem to fit your situation best.

The difference between what it costs to go to school and what you are expected to pay is known in the trade as the financial gap. File for aid to close that gap in the form of a scholarship, a loan, a job—or some combination of the three. Maybe you'll get shut out entirely, but you can't lose anything by trying. There are plenty of other options you can sniff out on your own.

Essentially the question is one of raising the bridge, lowering the water—or both. Choosing a college ought not to depend only on money. Talent, taste, dreams, aspirations—the kind of intangibles money can't buy—deserve a lot of room to grow in. Everybody doesn't want to go to Harvard or Stanford, so maybe you can start by lowering the water. The comparatively low costs of a nearby commuter college, or a live-in state university might fill the bill.

Raise the bridge. Generate more resources on your own. Maybe it's time for the lady of the house to shuck her apron and get back into the market economy.

Maybe it's time to get some good after all out of that straight life insurance policy you shouldn't have bought in the first place. Borrow against it. Maybe there's enough equity in the house for you to refinance it.

If you can't shake the scholarship tree on campus, there are plenty of other places to try. Many companies have scholarship programs for employees' children. So do many unions. Many ethnic and fraternal organizations make a tremendous effort. The Elks, for example, are making a commitment of more than $650,000 a year in scholarships to students who have demonstrated excellence in school, leadership, or need. Write to the chairman of the B.P.O.E. Lodge in your town. Here are some other sources to comb in your search for help: *Scholarships, Fellowships and Loans* (Bellman Publishing Co., Arlington, Mass. 02174), and *Barron's Handbook of American College Financial Aid* (113 Crossways Park Drive, Woodbury, N.Y. 11797).

One of the very best strategy guides I have seen, succinct but loaded with valuable tips, is *Don't Miss Out, The Ambitious Student's Guide to Scholarships and Loans.* It is published by Octameron Associates, P.O. Box 3437, Alexandria, Va. 22302.

The Federal Government is a major source of help—from the five service academies (West Point, Annapolis, the Air Force, Coast Guard and Merchant Marine) and R.O.T.C. programs on out to nursing student programs. There are two major grant programs based on need—the Basic Educational Opportunity Grant and the Supplemental Educational

Opportunity Grant. The Federal Government also subsidizes the college work-study program which provides on and off campus jobs for students who demonstrate great financial need. For more information, check guidance counselors, libraries, or write directly for a fact sheet on the loan and grant programs to the Department of Health, Education and Welfare, Office of Education, Washington, D.C. 20202.

All of the states offer a potpourri of grants, scholarships, loans and tuition assistance plans. It helps to be poor, gifted, or interested in some thinly populated specialized field. One good source on what the states are doing is "Need a Lift?" The booklet is available from the American Legion, National Emblem Sales, P.O. Box 1055, Indianapolis, Ind. 46206. For closer-to-home sources of help, try your local Chamber of Commerce, and keep an eye on the newspapers for intelligence on what your hometown clubs and associations might be doing.

If all else fails—if your children are not super-smart, super-athletic, super-poor or super-lucky—there is always the much-maligned guaranteed student loan program. It has been much maligned because many of the scare headlines about high loan delinquency rates have made it look as though we've raised a generation of super-deadbeats. The problem is as heavy and rich as grandma's fruitcake, with plenty of blame to go around for everyone. Some students are outright gonifs, it's true, but H.E.W. has never been famous for its administrative skills, and some bankers—rather than go to the expense of using commercial collection practices—found it cheaper to dump the defaults in Washington's lap.

Many banks, in fact, have used the delinquency figures as an excuse for limiting the number of student loans they are willing to make, and often as an excuse for not making the loans at all. For much of the middle class, however, the program is a godsend.

You don't have to establish need for a guaranteed loan, no matter how much money you make. With some exceptions, it used to be that only students from families with gross income of less than $25,000 were entitled during their school years to a subsidy on the 7 percent interest charge. That is no longer the case. The government now picks up the tab no matter what the income level, and will continue to do so until nine to 12 months after graduation. At that point, the student is supposed to work out a repayment schedule with the lender.

The size of the payments are keyed to the amount of debt and the student's ability to repay. A student who has found a good job immediately after graduation is obviously expected to pay off the loan more quickly than one who is still settling into the labor market.

In most cases, the lender will expect to get back a minimum of $360 a year at first, but the repayment period can be stretched to as long as 10 years. The bank is insured against default by the Feds and State agencies. You can borrow up to $2,500 a year for a maximum of $7,500 as an undergraduate; as much as $5,000 a year for graduate or professional study, up to a maximum of $15,000. That figure includes under-graduate loans.

One way of easing the loan burden is to start saving early. You can do so, and get a bit of a tax break, by opening a custodial savings account for a child. Since his own tax bracket is likely to come under the heading of *de minimis*, the interest build-up in the account is tax-free—so long as you don't convert the money to your own use. Another way of doing the same thing with probably a higher overall rate of return but at somewhat higher risk is to buy stock in a company with a dividend reinvestment plan—preferably one where the reinvestment buys stock at a discount. It, too, should go into a custody account so the I.R.S. can't zap you for the dividends.

If you've got a big bunch of money or stock kicking around that you absolutely won't have to touch for a long time—at least 10 years and one day, to be exact—maybe you can exorcise the demon bursar with the incense of a Clifford Trust. The dividend stream goes tax-free to the beneficiary and should, over the 10-year period of the turst, generate enough cash to at least help with the textbooks.

You can name yourself as trustee at some savings in fees and you can reclaim your assets, at no tax liability, when the trust self-destructs. There are some technicalities—possible gift taxes, for one, depending on how much you put in trust. Talk over the details with your lawyer, accountant or banker. They will welcome you. After all, they too, poor fellows, may have kids to put through college.

TOP DOLLAR TIPS

(1)   Expect the colleges to make you contribute more than you ever expected to your childrens' education.

(2)   Having your child declare "financial independence" in the hope of attracting financial aid is probably self-defeating, and may cost you a useful tax exemption to boot.

(3)   Some places to shake the scholarship tree—the company you work for; your union; fraternal organizations like the Elks.

(4)   Put a high priority on sniffing out scholarships and grants. They don't have to be paid back. Loans do.

Chapter 6

Asserting Your Consumer Rights

For all the manifest improvements in consumer protection that have been packed into the statute books over the last couple of years, it is increasingly clear that some things cannot be legislated. One of those things, perhaps as uneradicable as human nature itself, is gullibility.

It's not just the victims of three-card monte, Spanish prisoner, and bank examiner scams so beloved by tabloid newspaper editors. Or even the peddlers of moose pasture real estate, who hope to bait you with a free dinner and a lot of technicolor hype on the glories of leisure in the boonies. You can even think of the dynamiters peddling diamonds or solar heating by telephone as one with those hard-breathing roofing and siding salesmen. They're all throwbacks to the snake oil days of industrial capitalism. The easy option is to hang up the phone. If you let yourself get taken, it may simply be that like most marks, you've got a touch of larceny in your own soul.

There are still plenty of fast-talking conmen around, heaven knows. But much of the stuff that keeps cropping up in the complaint files of consumer protection agencies reflects not so much outright charlatanry as inadequate research or vincible ignorance on the part of the buyer.

As much as 10 percent of the work load of many such agencies, for example, revolves around the purchase of new or secondhand automobiles. True, the literature is full of blood-curdling tales of auto salesmen who will warm up a prospect with a "low ball" offer on one model, and then steer him in the direction of something higher priced. There are indeed dealers who will load a car with unordered options on the hope that the buyer will be too hopped up with enthusiasm to walk away from the higher price on delivery date. There are indeed also dealers who will try to fatten their profit margins by extra billing on "preparatory" work that never gets done.

The dealers themselves, of course, insist that the number of atrocity stories is grossly exaggerated. Perhaps it is. The tales of rapacity are deeply enough embedded in the folklore, however, to keep the prudent buyer from being overly complacent in what may well prove to be enemy territory. Any major purchase should be looked on as an adversary proceeding: the dealer wants to sell at as high a price as he can; you want to buy at as low a price as you can.

Probably the best place to start looking for a new car is not in the clamor of a showroom, but in the quiet of your living room or a library. First, a couple of preliminaries. How much car do you need? How much do you want to spend? You can translate those variables into a relatively narrow number of choices by thumbing through the comprehensive list of new models published every year by two excellent magazines—*Consumer Reports* and *Changing Times. Consumer Reports* goes more deeply into individual model performance than *CT*, but both publications provide such basic statistics as size, weight, engine capacity, and the like.

Equally important, both publications list the dealer cost and suggested list prices on all major models and options. Still another source of the same information is *Edmond's New Car Prices* (Dell).

On some imported cars, there is no give at all, but a fix on the dealer's cost is the basic point from which you should bargain. It's good business to work on the assumption that the dealer is entitled to a profit. If he doesn't get it up front, there is every reason to suspect that he will get it behind your back. Shop at least three dealers, and make sure they're all talking about the same thing.

Consumer Reports notes, for example, that dealer preparation costs of $25 to $75 are "typical" on most imports, but may run to as much as "$100 or even $200" on more expensive models. "Before you agree to a deal," urges *Consumer Reports,* "make sure you know how much the dealer intends to charge for preparation and consider it part of the dealer's profit."

On most domestic models, somewhere in the $125 to $300 range above cost is a fair dealer profit. Perhaps you'd rather stay out of the cross-fire entirely and let a middleman do the bargaining for you. Consider the possibility of working through either Car/Puter International Corp., 1603 Bushwick Ave., Brooklyn, N.Y. 11207, or Computerized Car Costs Co., 14411 W. Eight Mile Road, Detroit, Mich. 48235. Both concerns, for a very modest charge, will supply a readout showing dealer's cost on any auto model and/or options you select. Both companies also stand ready to deliver through participating dealers most new model cars at $125 over dealer's cost—a real buy if you don't have to pick up your purchase in Detroit. Make sure the dealer is located close enough to home for convenience and servicing.

The servicing is important, at least through the warranty period. That's why it's important to check out a dealer's reputation before you buy. Talk to friends, check out your local consumer affairs department for complaints. You can get a more general rundown by taking a look at *Consumer Reports'* dealer service charts, a distillation of reader opinions on such meaningful characteristics as charges and adequacy of repair.

You might just be willing to go up a bit on price with a dealer who has a reputation for quality service than with one who does not. Above all, don't let yourself get rushed. Spot delivery can be a trap. It may be a great ego trip to drive out of the showroom with an impulse purchase, but a new car represents too big an item these days to do anything on the spur of the moment.

A new car depreciates about 50 percent in the first two years of its life, and you absorb almost the first 25 percent of that the first time you get behind the wheel. The depreciation timetable, in fact, is one of the reasons why many challenge the conventional wisdom that the best buys can be had in the late summer and early fall, just before the new models make their debut.

It is true that there are some bargains to be had then, but count on hanging on to such a purchase for at least three or four years—long enough for the quick depreciation induced by the advent of the new models to even out. Many revisionists argue that the best time to buy is actually in January and February—after the hoopla over the new models has died down, and the dead hand of winter has begun to set in on the dealer's inventory.

In general, you are better off at any time of year financing your purchase through a bank or a credit union than through a dealer. The interest rate is almost invariably lower, and there are virtues to keeping the deal uncluttered so that you can concentrate on getting the best buy.

If you're thinking about trading in your old car, for example, don't drag that possibility into the bargaining until you've established what the dealer's last price on the new car is. After you've pinned down the price on a naked deal, start talking trade-in, if you want to. Keeping the two items separate gives you the tactical upper hand. It stymies the tired old ploy of the handsome-looking offer on the old car that gets offset by an equally handsome boost on the price of the new car.

Dealers are the same everywhere. Their living comes from buying wholesale and selling retail. You fare best at somewhere around the midpoint of those two lines. Selling a used car on your own can be time-consuming and inconvenient, but doing so is often the best way to go.

For that matter, why not consider a used car instead of a new model, particularly if you're in the market for a second car? Prices tend to be higher on new car lots, mainly because the dealers tend to keep for resale only the best iron they've taken on trade-in. Straight-out used car dealers often draw much of their stock from auctions. It takes a discerning eye and good mechanical sense to distinguish value from a gas-guzzling pig in a poke.

One source of quality secondhand cars to check out: the big rental agencies—Hertz and Avis, among others. You can get a good feel for wholesale and retail prices from the monthly National Automobile Dealers Association Official Used Car Guide. *Consumer Reports'* frequency-of-repairs records can give you a line on the sort of mechanical problems to which you might fall heir.

One advantage to opting for a used car is lower insurance costs, no small advantage in a period of super heated premium increases. Unless you're driving an extremely costly used car, you probably won't need collision coverage at all—protection that could cost anywhere from $250 a year on up in many states.

Nor, with a used car, will you need to carry as much comprehensive coverage, which is designed to reimburse you for such non-collision hazards as fire, theft, vandalism, storm and wind damage. Otherwise, though, it's prudent to stick with the same basic insurance package you'd buy on a new car. The package should include these elements:

Liability protection covering death or bodily injury on the one hand, and property damage on the other. In the shorthand of the industry, the level of liability protection might be expressed cabalistically as 50/100/10. That means the insurance company will pay up to a maximum of $50,000 for injury to one person; $100,000 maximum for all others injured in the same accident; and up to $10,000 worth of property damage. In these litigious, inflationary times 100/300/10 ($100,000 for one person; $300,000 for all persons and so on) coverage is an absolute minimum. If you own a house or any other visible assets and make a pretty good salary, consider jacking your policy limits to 300/500/10. The cost will be more, but not all that much more, and perhaps you can economize elsewhere.

Collision coverage is a necessity on a new car, but can be phased out once the book value of the vehicle drops to modest levels. You can cut the cost of collision coverage by taking the maximum deduction of $250. The company won't pay off until you've absorbed more than $250 worth of damage, but remember that there's another party involved—Uncle Sam. Any casualty loss of more than $100—including a damaged car—is tax deductible. The higher your tax bracket, the more sense it makes to go for the higher deductible.

Two other elements common to the traditional standard auto policy cover medical treatment and damages done by uninsured (or inadequately insured) motorists. More than half of the states have shifted to a "no fault" system of insurance, designed to limit costly courtroom determinations of who was "negligent" in an accident. No negligence, no payment, is the old tort rule.

Under no-fault, you look to your own company for reimbursement. You buy insurance to protect yourself, and not for protection from the other guy's lawyers. All of the no fault states require wage loss coverage, designed to compensate for an injury-enforced stay away from the job.

The amount of cash you have to shell out for auto insurance varies with a lot more than just the amount of protection you want to take on. The kind of car you drive, the sort of driving you do (business or pleasure), age, sex, and safety record all have an important impact on rates. Insurance companies tend to file their rates in packs, and rarely do any promotional selling on the basis of price. The competition is there, though, especially for good risks—over age 25 motorists with clean driving records. Thus, it pays to shop. In general, companies that sell through a commission-oriented agency system charge higher rates than companies such as All State and State

Farm, which direct sell through a captive sales force.

The jockeying for low risk policyholders is so intense that many motorists have trouble getting protection at standard rates. If you feel that you've been discriminated against, or arbitrarily canceled out of a policy, take your complaint to the State Insurance Commissioner's Office. Put your case in writing. Most Commissioners are located in the state capital, and many have consumer affairs departments assigned to do nothing but grapple with citizens' squawks.

Before trying to infiltrate the bureaucracy, though, there is something to be said for exhausting your remedies with the company involved; and that holds not only for insurance, but for any other kind of gripe as well—automobiles, appliances, electric trains or radar-operated bidets.

Government, of course, has no monopoly on bureaucracy. Corporations can be great heaving wastelands of unresponsive jelly, too. Start with the corporate manifestation closest to you. Telephone, and ask specifically for the name of the person who handles problems of the sort that's bugging you—a broken warranty, for example, a late delivery, a bad billing, or whatever. Explain the difficulty as temperately as you can, and follow up with a letter recapping the conversation. Keep the carbon. If you still get no action, fire off a letter to the president of the company (dig his name out of Standard & Poor's Directory of Officers and Directors at the library), with carbon copies and a formal complaint to your local consumer affairs agency.

Consumer affairs agencies come in all shapes and

sizes. Some operate on a city level, some on a county level, some on the state level. Some have very strong regulatory powers, others almost none beyond the power of persuasion. The best idea is to start on the level nearest you, where you can probably get some leverage going for you—if needed—with the help of a ward leader, councilman, or any other politico who comes looking for your help on election day.

Groping for quasi-political solutions to what is basically a commercial problem doesn't recommend itself, but some businessmen are totally insensitive to any other kind of heat. Extreme circumstances sometimes demand extreme measures. Doing something is one helluva lot better than being a sheep.

One of big problems is where to make yourself heard. Many consumer complaint agencies lack visibility, according to a study done not long ago by the Center for Study of Responsive Law. Check under local or county government headings for Consumer Affairs or some variation on the title in the telephone book. Write the Consumer Federation of America (1012 14th Street, N.W., Washington, D.C. 20005) for its *Directory of State and Local Consumer Groups.*

Consider taking your complaint to a Better Business Bureau. They are not the most aggressive consumer advocates in the world, but the B.B.B.s are trying to sharpen up their act. Many offer arbitration services that can prove helpful. Too, some industry groups have set up consumer mediation panels. They are not binding on members, but can sometimes be helpful.

If you've got a complaint about a major appliance,

for example, write to the Major Appliance Consumer Action Panel (MACAP) at 20 N. Wacker Drive, Chicago, Ill. 60606. Explain your problem and where the impasse lies. MACAP, in turn, will get the manufacturer's side of the argument. If the producer doesn't agree to settle, the mediators will try to work out a solution.

Local automobile dealers associations, under the aegis of the National Association of Automobile Dealers Association, are also in the process of putting together a mediation service.

If all of the good guy stuff we've gone through so far doesn't bring relief, escalate! Consider bringing a suit in Small Claims Court, which you can find under the city or county government heading in the phone book. The courts are informal, the procedures simple, the cost nominal, and the results often entertaining, if nothing else.

There are other alternatives—a host of Federal agencies that regulate everything from air transport and the moving industry to ethical drug producers and railroads. For help in finding out which branch of what agency can help you, try the Federal Information Centers listed by states below:

FEDERAL INFORMATION CENTERS

ARIZONA

PHOENIX
(602) 261-3313
Federal Building
230 N. 1st Ave.
85025

CALIFORNIA

LOS ANGELES
(213) 688-3800
Federal Building
300 N. Los Angeles St.
90012

SACRAMENTO
(916) 440-3344
Federal Building
650 Capitol Mall
95814

SAN DIEGO
(714) 293-6030
202 C St. 92101

SAN FRANCISCO
(415) 556-6600
Federal Building
450 Golden Gate Ave.
94102

COLORADO

DENVER
(303) 837-3602
Federal Building
1961 Stout St.
80202

DISTRICT OF
COLUMBIA

WASHINGTON
(202) 755-8660
7th & D Sts. S.W.
20407

FLORIDA

MIAMI
(305) 350-4155
Federal Building
51 S.W. 1st Ave. 33130

ST. PETERSBURG
(813) 893-3495
Federal Building
144 1st Ave. S. 33701

GEORGIA

ATLANTA
(404) 526-6891
Federal Building
275 Peachtree St. N.E.
30303

HAWAII

HONOLULU
(808) 546-8620
U.S. Post Office
335 Merchant St. 96813

ILLINOIS

CHICAGO
(312) 353-4242
Everett McKinley
  Dirksen Building
219 S. Dearborn St.
60604

INDIANA

INDIANAPOLIS
(317) 269-7373
Federal Building
575 N. Pennsylvania St.
46204

KENTUCKY

LOUISVILLE
(502) 582-6261
Federal Building
600 Federal Place
40202

LOUISIANA

NEW ORLEANS
(504) 589-6696
Federal Building
701 Loyola Ave. 70113

MARYLAND

BALTIMORE
(301) 962-4980
Federal Building
31 Hopkins Plaza
21201

MASSACHUSETTS

BOSTON
(617) 223-7121
John F. Kennedy
Federal Building
Government Center
02203

MICHIGAN

DETROIT
(313) 226-7016
Federal Building
447 Michigan Ave.
48226

MINNESOTA

MINNEAPOLIS
(612) 725-2073
Federal Building
110 S. 4th St. 55401

MISSOURI

KANSAS CITY
(816) 374-2466
Federal Building
601 E. 12th St. 64106

ST. LOUIS
(314) 425-4106
Federal Building
1520 Market St.
63103

NEBRASKA

OMAHA
(402) 221-3353
Federal Building
215 N. 17th St. 68102

NEW JERSEY

NEWARK
(201) 645-3600
Federal Building
970 Broad St. 07102

NEW MEXICO

ALBUQUERQUE
(505) 766-3091
Federal Building
500 Gold Ave. S.W.
87101

NEW YORK

BUFFALO
(716) 842-5770
Federal Building
111 W. Huron St. 14202

NEW YORK
(212) 264-4464
Federal Office Building
26 Federal Plaza 10007

OHIO

CINCINNATI
(513) 684-2801
Federal Building
550 Main St. 45202

CLEVELAND
(216) 522-4040
Federal Building
1240 E. 9th St. 44199

OKLAHOMA

OKLAHOMA CITY
(405) 231-4868
Federal Office Building
201 N.W. 3rd St. 73102

OREGON

PORTLAND
(503) 221-2222
Federal Building
1220 S.W. 3rd Ave.
97204

PENNSYLVANIA

PHILADELPHIA
(215) 597-7042
Federal Building
600 Arch St. 19106

PITTSBURGH
(412) 644-3456
Federal Building
1000 Liberty Ave. 15222

TENNESSEE

MEMPHIS
(901) 534-3285
Federal Building
167 N. Main St. 38103

TEXAS

FORT WORTH
(817) 334-3624
Federal Building
819 Taylor St. 76102

HOUSTON
(713) 226-5711
Federal Building
515 Rusk Ave. 77002

UTAH

SALT LAKE CITY
(801) 524-5353
Federal Building
125 S. State St. 84138

WASHINGTON

SEATTLE
(206) 442-0570
Federal Building
915 2nd Ave. 98174

Residents of the following 38 cities can call the local number given and get a toll-free tieline to the nearest information center:

ALABAMA

BIRMINGHAM
322-8591

MOBILE 438-1421

ARIZONA

TUCSON 622-1511

ARKANSAS

LITTLE ROCK 378-6177

CALIFORNIA

SAN JOSE 275-7422

COLORADO

COLORADO SPRINGS
471-9491

PUEBLO 544-9523

CONNECTICUT

HARTFORD 527-2617

NEW HAVEN 624-4720

FLORIDA

FORT LAUDERDALE
522-8531

JACKSONVILLE
354-4756

TAMPA 229-7911

WEST PALM BEACH
833-7566

IOWA

DES MOINES 282-9091

KANSAS

TOPEKA 232-7229

WICHITA 263-6931

MISSOURI

ST. JOSEPH 233-8206

NEW JERSEY

TRENTON 396-4400

NEW MEXICO

SANTA FE 983-7743

NEW YORK

ALBANY 463-4421

ROCHESTER 546-5075

SYRACUSE 476-8545

NORTH CAROLINA

CHARLOTTE 376-3600

OHIO

AKRON 375-5475

COLUMBUS 221-1014

DAYTON 223-7377

TOLEDO 244-8625

OKLAHOMA

TULSA 548-4193

PENNSYLVANIA

SCRANTON 346-7081

RHODE ISLAND

PROVIDENCE 331-5565

TENNESSEE

CHATTANOOGA
265-8231

NASHVILLE 242-5056

TEXAS

AUSTIN 472-5494

DALLAS 749-2131

SAN ANTONIO 224-4471

UTAH

OGDEN 399-1347

WASHINGTON

TACOMA 383-5230

WISCONSIN

MILWAUKEE 271-2273

TOP DOLLAR TIPS

*(1) Buying a car? Do some library research with
Consumer Reports and Changing Times before tack-
ling the showrooms.*

*(2) Cut automobile insurance costs by electing high
deductibles.*

(3) Got a consumer complaint? Make it in writing, keep a carbon, follow up.

(4) If necessary, use political leverage to ease you through the bureaucracy of tax-supported consumer complaint agencies.

HOW TO PROTECT YOUR ASSETS

Chapter 7

Life Insurance

Life insurance is a key defensive element in your money management planning. For anyone who has dependents or an estate to protect against the ravages of time or the income tax, it is good Clausewitzian doctrine to "Secure the Home Base." So preached the Prussian strategist, and he was right.

Paradoxically, though, a number of studies—including one done not long ago by the University of Minnesota—suggest that nearly one out of every two American families is "seriously underinsured."

One reason for the shortfall may be the way the industry itself works. The practice varies, but most insurance salesmen and agents are paid on a commission basis. Thus, there is a built-in bias for the men on the firing line (who have families of their own to protect) to push the most expensive lines of coverage (ordinary, or "whole" life and the many variations on it), while playing down or absolutely bad-mouthing the much cheaper term insurance.

Ordinary insurance accumulates cash surrender values. Term insurance, on the other hand, offers no cash values—often called "living values" in the sales spiel—and must be thought of as pure protection. For some people, ordinary insurance may be the better buy. For most though, particularly young families, term is the best bet. Unfortunately, the commission incentives are all the other way.

As Michael A. Pascale, a general agent for the International Insurance Co. of Buffalo, told a *Money* magazine seminar: "If I sell this $25,000 straight life policy, I make 55 percent commission. If I sell term, I make 25 percent. So I'm going to do all I can to sell that straight life."

Mr. Pascale's point was that the insurance companies ought to take some of the bias out of the sales pitch by equalizing commissions, and paying their agents as much for selling term insurance as they do any other kind. A few companies have begun to do just that, but most are hanging on to the old ways.

Thus, striking a compromise between their needs and what they can afford, many couples wind up being sold modest amounts of high cost ordinary insurance when for the same amount of money they could have bought a much larger amount of term insurance.

I emphasize the verb "sold." Otherwise knowledgeable people often get so bogged down in the mysteries of the product that they really can't be said to be buyers in the strict sense of the word. They are sold.

Take the case of the couple whom in this account I'll call Al and Kate. Last year a salesman talked them into buying about $11,000 worth of ordinary insurance on each of them at a total cost of $30 a month.

Al and Kate are in their late 20s, and have already started a family. Both were working at the time they bought the insurance, but it was clear at the time that Al was likely to be the family's principal breadwinner for a long time to come. In retrospect, Al thinks it might have been smarter to put more of the insurance on himself and less on Kate. "We didn't think of it in terms of earning power," said Al. "We just wanted to be fair."

The reach for equity rather than economics, loving as it was, is just one more sign of the emotional pressures that often get in the way of buying insurance. Facing the certainty of one's own death, however theoretically, does not always permit rational choices.

The salesman, even though his business card identified him as a "financial planner," wasn't much help. He never raised the question of who should be carrying how much coverage, and he certainly never posed the alternative of buying term coverage.

The model sales code promulgated by the National Association of Insurance Commissioners requires salesmen to spell out the differences between term insurance, whole life and such other variants as endowment policies. All life insurance contracts agree to pay off a certain sum if you die, but they differ in material respects. The differences determine how much you pay and what you get.

Term policies, as the name suggests, cover periods of one or more years (generally five), and are renewable for one or more terms without the need to go through a physical or furnish any other proof of "insurability." There are no cash values, but besides being renewable, the best term policies permit you to convert to a permanent form of insurance whenever you choose to do so, generally up to age 60 or 65.

The premiums on term policies continue to rise with every renewal because you are actuarially just that much closer to your last breath and the point at which the insurance company will have to pay off on your beneficiaries' claim.

The premiums on ordinary insurance, on the other hand, are level—they remain the same for as long as the policy is in force. There is nothing constant, however, about the way the payments are earmarked. In the early years, a big chunk of them goes out in commissions and other administrative costs.

For convenience sake, think of the premiums as having two components—one covering death benefits as such, the other covering the savings or investment feature of the policy. The cash build-up —which you can borrow against at comparatively low rates (see Chapter 8) or collect on by turning in the policy—is very slow in the early years of the contract. Because of the level premium, you pay comparatively more for protection at first because the company has to set aside a reserve against the time later on when the odds on your dying increase.

The salesman leaned heavily on the cash build-up in his pitch to Al and Kate. If you put it all together, over a 20-year period, he said—subtract the cash values and the dividends the company would be paying from the premiums—the net cost of the policy would be practically zero.

Al liked the prospect of a low cost package he could borrow against if need be, and he liked the thought of the long term cash build-up being a kind of forced saving. He should have checked the figures more closely. At age 30, a $10,000 ordinary life policy typically will cost Al about $191 a year and Kate $180.90 a year. A five-year renewable term will cost them about $48.10 and $45.60, respectively—roughly one-fourth less for the same amount of coverage. To turn the equation around, Al and Kate could have bought at least four times as much term protection for the cash they're putting into ordinary life insurance.

True, the cost of term will continue rising with each renewal. But term insurance is often the only way young people on tight budgets can buy a respectable amount of protection when they most need it—the period in which the children are growing up. Further, as in Al's case, the slope of the insurance costs will rise pretty much in train with the pay increases he expects as he moves on in his profession.

The rather steep climb in premiums is one of the reasons why many insurance salesmen insist that ordinary life is absolutely the best buy. And it is certainly true that out around age 60 or so, term premiums can look prohibitive. But at that age, a person may be able to do with less insurance or drop the coverage entirely because: (a) the dependents have all flown the nest, or (b) the family has accumulated enough other assets to compensate for any loss in earning power. Further, there is always the option of converting to a smaller amount of ordinary life.

Thus, for many individuals term insurance is a very flexible tool. It dovetails nicely with the life cycle. Declining term insurance, for example—a policy that drops from $30,000 to zero over a 20-year period, say—can be used to cover such declining balance obligations as mortgages or college loans. Term is ideally suited for such temporary needs.

That's not to say ordinary life or endowment policies are without utility. If you've got permanent needs—the need to cover estate taxes, for example—a permanent form of insurance is the best answer. Ordinary coverage, thanks to its forced saving feature, may also be helpful to people who find themselves constitutionally incapable of putting money away in any other fashion. Ordinary coverage, because of the tax shelter it offers, can also be helpful in high income brackets. The cash values build year by year, and are taxable only if the policy is discontinued. Even then the tax liability extends only to the excess of cash value over premiums.

If you're thinking of insurance as a savings vehicle or a tax shelter, though, make sure the policy can stand on its own two feet. It has to be compared with the risks and rewards of other forms of savings, investment and tax shelter—long term time deposits, common stocks and municipal bonds, for example.

Over 20 years, the savings in a whole life policy probably earn between 4 percent and 5 percent at minuscule risk. The net return varies with the cost of the policy and the buyer's tax bracket. For most, the return doesn't stack up with the competition, especially if you take inflation into account. You pay your premiums in current dollars, get paid back in depreciated dollars. That's good for the company, not so good for you.

On that basis alone, it's better to buy protection at the cheapest rate you can find, and finesse the possibility of letting youself get diverted by peripheral values. Think of insurance in terms of its primary function, which is to compensate for a loss in earning power.

The size of that potential loss is a key factor in figuring how much life insurance you should carry. Ideally, the policy should generate enough capital to cover your salary, to take care of funeral and other windup expenses, and maybe cover the mortgage.

For many, that goal is out of reach. It takes a little over $415,000 at 6 percent interest, for example, to produce $25,000 a year. That is a lot of insurance. Who can afford that much? Many companies will very happily provide worksheets and computer programs to help you estimate your needs—happily because the programming is a useful selling tool.

One important thing to remember is that those needs vary all over the lot, and change as circumstances change. Does an unmarried working woman or man really need much more than a modest amount of insurance? Not unless they've got dependent parents to think about, or would like to provide some posthumous help for a favorite niece's education. The same can be said for couples who don't plan to have any children. The cash that would be going into premiums can be earmarked for more rewarding forms of investment.

Married couples with small children, or households in which the wife makes a significant contribution to income, on the other hand, should do some serious thinking about how much coverage to buy for the woman. What kind of economic value should be assigned to cooking and cleaning, the care and feeding of youngsters? What would it cost to hire even a part-time replacement? If there is a heavy mortgage that can be paid off only with the help of two paychecks, the insurance equation should take that into account, too. Circumstances invariably shape family needs. The peak comes during the 10- to 20-year period when the wife's earning power may be truncated by the responsibilities of caring for growing children. Generally, that is also the period when the college tuition bills start rolling in. From the mid-50s on out, the curve begins to drop.

At almost every point along the curve, though, there is continuing tension between what the family might need and what it can afford. According to a table prepared by the Bankers Life Co. of Des Moines, Iowa, a 35-year-old man with four children making $20,000 a year would need about $114,000 worth of insurance—in addition to Social Security benefits—

to replace 75 percent of his after-tax earnings on out to age 65. A one year term policy for that much money would cost about $540, or 2.7 percent of gross income.

In the end, what you need almost invariably shakes down to what you can afford, and at first inspection, the gap is likely to seem unbridgeable. Social Security benefits, however, are an enormous help. They go on until the youngest child is 18 and continue beyond that point if he or she is in college.

The one problem with Social Security is the so-called Widow's Blackout—the period between when benefits on the youngest child end and the point at which the widow becomes eligible for Social Security on her own. The depth of the blackout depends to some degree on the widow's earning power. If she has marketable work skills, the blackout may not be a problem at all. If getting a decent job is likely to be a poser, take that prospect into account. In the later years of the life cycle, it might mean stretching out a big chunk of coverage for a longer period of time instead of cutting back.

How much insurance you can afford is partly a function of its cost. The business of comparing costs—shopping—is complicated not only by the level of premiums, but by such other variables as cash values and dividends. Cost is no idle question. There are wide differences between companies. At this writing, for example, the 20-year average gross premium for a 35-year-old male on $10,000 worth of whole life coverage bought from American Republic Life of New York is $17.09 per thousand. Security Life of New York, on the other hand, according to a survey by the

New York State Insurance Department, carries a 20-year average gross premium of $27.76 per thousand. That is a spread of more than 50 percent.

Variations from company to company are hard enough to fathom, but there are even variations within the same company, depending on the kind of policy you buy. Rates tend to be lower on larger policies than on smaller ones, for example, and a younger person is likely to get a larger discount on a big policy than an older person.

Cost comparisons are straightforward enough when you're dealing with non-participating term insurance—coverage which by definition accumulates neither cash values nor the dividends paid on "participating" policies. The bottom line is easy to find. If you're thinking in terms of a 20-year spectrum, just multiply the annual premium by the number of years involved. If you're dealing with five-year terms, remember that the premium is going to climb at the end of each of those increments because statistically you are just that much closer to being dead.

You want a policy that is renewable (one that continues automatically at the end of every term without the need to go through another physical) and convertible (one that can be switched to whole life if you choose to do so). Once you've done the arithmetic, you'll see that the cost differences between companies even on the Model A of the line—term insurance—can be striking, sometimes as much as 40 percent over a 20-year period.

The arithmetic isn't always that simple. Some term policies pay dividends. Indeed, all coverage written by mutual (non-stockholder owned) companies is "participating" in the sense that the mutuals are required to distribute any surplus they make over operating costs and reserves to policyholders. To stay competitive with the mutuals, many stockholder-owned companies also sell participating policies.

The important thing to remember is that the dividends paid on policies are in effect a return of premium. The premiums on participating policies are almost invariably higher than on non-participating coverage. The dividends can be used to reduce premiums or earmarked to buy additional protection. The question of whether a participating policy in the end costs less than non-participating coverage, however, is a very hot statistical potato to juggle.

For one thing, you have to crank into the reckoning an imputed interest cost on the extra premiums you've been laying out. A similar adjustment has to be made for the cash value build-up in whole life. After all, the additional cash you've been paying out over and above the cost of pure protection, could have been earning at least 5 percent in a savings account.

Dividend payouts vary considerably. They are the product, among other things, of a company's mortality experience and the size of the return it is getting on its own investment portfolio. Some policies begin to pay comparatively good dividends early on in the cycle, others not until much later. Apples and oranges. What is needed is a formula that would iron out those differences and thus make it possible to weigh the cost of specific kinds of policies at specific points in time.

The formula—the so-called interest-adjusted method—was years in the making and to some degree is still swathed in controversy. It may be a poor tool in some respects, but it's the only one we've got to gauge costs on a reasonably comparable basis. The formula works on index numbers. The lower the index number, the cheaper the policy. The comparison has to be quite specific. Match up the companies only in terms of the kind of policy you want to buy, the amount you want to buy, and your age.

The index is a skeleton key, but it opens only one door at a time. As the National Association of Insurance Commissioners notes, "Just because a 'shopper's guide' tells you that one company's policy is a good buy for a particular age and amount, you should not assume that all of that company's policies are equally good buys."

The N.A.I.C. helped to midwife the shopper's guide. In some states, the salesman is required by law to make the guide available to prospects. Any reputable agent should be willing to produce one on request. Make sure, though, that you're getting a full rundown on all the companies licensed to do business in your state, and not just a cross-section that might have the effect of limiting your choice.

One of the choices you will have to make is the same kind you face in an automobile showroom—do you want a stripped-down "straight six" or something with some options on it. As with an automobile, the options—called riders—add to your costs.

Three of the most common riders are waiver of premium disability benefits, disability income benefits, and accidental death (double or triple indemnity) benefits. The waiver of premium option is so useful that some companies include it in their basic policies at no extra costs.

Waiver provisions vary, but in general they wipe out the obligation to continue paying premiums for any policyholder who has been permanently disabled for six (sometimes four) months. Most such policies also retroactively refund any payments made after the beginning of the disability. The cost is modest and a worthwhile investment. The waiver is a kind of disability insurance. In effect, it is a separate policy designed to keep your basic protection intact if you can no longer work.

The waiver, though, is different from another rider that will pay so much a month—$10 per thousand is the most common arrangement—if permanent disability strikes. For reasons spelled out in the next chapter, you are probably better off giving the disability rider the go-by and buying such coverage as a separate policy.

Professional groups (medical and bar associations, among others), alumni associations, credit unions, and credit card companies are just a few of the outlets where very low cost renewable term life insurance can be found. Not-for-profit fraternal groups are also often a good place to look. A number of mutual funds—all of the investment companies managed by the Dreyfus Corporation, for example—also sell very cheap coverage.

Nobody's giving anything away. There are economies of scale in any group operation of course, and maybe there is a little money to be made, but the life insurance is essentially a sales tool. Credit card companies—American Express and Master Charge, for example—like to hang on to their customers. So do mutual funds. You're entitled to the low group premium only for as long as you remain a member of the group, though generally the coverage can be converted to an individual policy at a higher rate if you leave. Thus, group life is often a kind of sweetener designed to keep turnover among the clientele down, but that doesn't make it any less a good buy. Group rates vary every bit as much as the premiums on individual policies, though, and so—as always—it pays to shop.

As for accidental death benefit riders, the less said the better. Thanks to James M. Cain's novel, double indemnity's place in fiction and film is secure. In real life the option, which pays off twice the face value of the policy if you die in something so messy as a car or plane accident, doesn't make very much sense. It's a gamble. If you like the doubling feature because you're not carrying enough insurance to begin with, you're better off taking the cost of the option and buying more coverage with it.

Where is the cheapest coverage to be found? If you live or work in New York, Connecticut or Massachusetts, take a look at the insurance sold by savings banks. It includes some of the lowest cost protection around. Think about joining a group, too. Coverage bought through a group is almost invariably cheaper than insurance bought on an individual basis. Employers are the most common source of that kind of protection, but the group concept is an elastic one.

TOP DOLLAR TIPS

(1)   Term insurance is absolutely the best buy for young people who need a lot of coverage.

(2)   Ordinary and other permanent forms of insurance are best for permanent needs—paying off the taxes on an estate, for example.

(3)   Insurance dividends are nice, but they are in effect a return of premium. Dividend paying policies are invariably more costly than those that do not pay dividends.

(4)   Ordinary life insurance offers only a meager investment return. If you want investment values, take your money elsewhere.

Chapter 8

Medical
and Disability
Insurance

Disaster is always something that happens to the
other guy. If you can hear the bullet, it doesn't have
your name on it. A lot of us have not been listening too
well lately. Something like 15 million American
adults are partially or totally disabled, victims all of
either serious accident or catastrophic illness.

It is a deadly combination that can wipe out years of
painfully accumulated assets. Medical costs generally have torn through the roof; partly because of
inflation, partly because of the proliferation of such
new-life extending but extraordinarily expensive
techniques as dialysis machines and open heart
surgery. You can almost rent the bridal suite at the

Hotel Plaza with the daily charge on a semi-private room at many big hospitals. Link the out-of-pocket costs of a major illness with long term disability and you've got a formula for financial disaster.

There is no way you can protect yourself totally against the freakish twist of chance—carcinogens that slip through a minute tear in the genetic fabric, a drunken driver who should have been on the other side of the road. The impact can be cushioned, though, by a realistic approach to the uses of major medical insurance and disability insurance.

Premiums are not cheap, and it goes without saying: Every dollar earmarked for defensive purposes is one less master plan dollar available for investing in earning assets that can provide you with freedom or pleasure. The key question is how to get more bang out of your insurance buck. The answer is hornbook management. Protect yourself against the really big risks, roll with the smaller ones as best you can.

With both medical and disability insurance this means that you will, in effect, swallow a "deductible." You will bear, say, the first $500 or $1,000 of major medical costs yourself before the burden shifts to the insurance company. The same is true of disability insurance. Instead of expecting payment to begin within a week or so of your being off the job, settle for maybe a 60-day, 90-day, a six-month (or even longer) "elimination" period.

By co-insuring yourself you either (a) save on premiums; (b) get more protection for your money; or (c) both. The savings vary from company to company, and it's hard to give any lasting examples because premiums and insurance products change all the time. By way of illustration, though, one accident/illness disability policy with a zero to seven day elimination period might cost a 35-year-old male about $160 a year. By extending the waiting period to 180 days, he could cut the premium to a little over $60 a year.

Savings of that scale are available all along the line in both disability and major medical coverage. The principle is inviolate: protect yourself against the big catastrophic losses that may never happen, grapple as best you can with the smaller ones that happen all the time. Almost anyone can sweat out the costs involved in a bout of flu; few can absorb without major third party help the debilitating drain of multiple sclerosis.

The size of the deductible you elect depends in good measure on the state of your finances. How big a doctor's bill can you manage before it really begins to hurt? How many paychecks can you afford to let slip by before that begins to hurt?

The answers may be "not much" and "not many," but consider the other lines of defense you have working for you. If you do become permanently disabled, you're entitled to Social Security benefits. Some states (including New York, New Jersey and California) have put in disability income plans of their own. Many employers, quite aside from the workmen's compensation insurance they are required to carry for people injured on the job, also offer group disability coverage.

Many such group policies are part of the collective bargaining package, and not always as generous as they might be. One common standard is two weeks full pay for every year of service, plus two weeks half-pay on the same seniority basis. Thus, if you're a long-timer, you may be in pretty good shape; less so if you're new on the job.

There are primary lines of defense that will help you narrow the gap on major medical insurance, too. Almost all of us carry some form of hospitalization coverage. Fewer of us carry medical protection, designed to cover treatment by a doctor at home or in a hospital, and fewer still carry surgical protection needed to help meet the cost of an operation.

Those three elements—hospital, medical, surgical—make up a basic package. The most familiar of those packages is merchandised by the not-for-profit Blue Cross/Blue Shield organizations, often under group programs sold to employer-employee benefit plans. Many such plans, because they are "free" or partly so because of employer contribution, leave people feeling complacent about the kind of protection they have. If it's good enough for the boss—or the union—it's good enough for me, the sentiment goes.

The intelligent thing to do is take a look at what you've got and see how far it will take you. Anyone whose basic coverage isn't beefed up with major medical protection in these days of $25,000-and-up illnesses is tempting the fates. Major medical picks up where the limits of the basic policies leave off.

Group premiums, of course, are lower than individual premiums. If major medical isn't part of the fringe benefits where you work, perhaps you can get a bunch of fellow employees together and work out something on your own with one of the insurance companies. Another alternative might lie with religious or fraternal groups. Most Blue Cross organizations sell individual major medical coverage and there are hundreds of commercial carriers in the field, as well. The fierce competitive jockeying and often conflicting promotional claims don't make shopping for major medical an easy task.

Costs, for example, vary not only with age but with sex. Women pay more for individual commercial coverage than men. The thesis is that they are hospitalized more frequently than men. Where you live is a factor, too. Medical costs are a good deal higher in New York City and Los Angeles than in Davenport, Iowa or in Billings, Mont. The size of the deductible and the quality of the benefits package, of course, also have a lot to do with cost.

The deductible, which starts at $100 with many of the most popular major medical policies, is usually coupled with a co-insurance factor. Typically that means the insurer will pick up 80 percent of the bill and you 20 percent of the bill after the deductible has been reached. Say you've run up a tab of $5,100. You absorb the first $100. The balance gets split $1,000 (20 percent) to you; $4,000 (80 percent) to the insurance carrier. Some policies carry 75 percent–25 percent co-insurance clauses, others go as high as 85 percent–15 percent.

In general, the higher the proportion the carrier assumes, the better off you are. But those numbers have to be looked at in terms of the entire package. Is there a cut-off on the co-insurance requirement? If so, where does it begin? With some of the best regarded policies, the co-insurance clause phases out after your contribution reaches $1,000. From that point on, the company pays all of the freight on the claim.

Premiums also vary with the way the deductibles are figured. Some companies give you a whole year in which to accumulate the $100 or whatever floor has been set in the policy. Others give you only three months. Thus, if you run up $95 worth of otherwise reimbursable expenses in one three-month period, the company owes you nothing. If you run up $125 worth of expenses in the next three-month period, the company is liable only for $25. The longer the accumulation period, the better the deal—but that, too, is a generalization that has to be looked at in the full context of the policy.

Many policies, for example, bristle with tough "internal limits" of, say, $150 a day for hospital accommodations, or $250 for a hernia operation. The policy will not pay off on anything above those flat dollar figures. Because of the horrendous rate at which medical costs are escalating, the carriers don't like to get themselves locked in. The fewer limits there are, the better off you are. Look particularly sharply at the maximum amounts a company will pay. They are sometimes parsed in terms of a lifetime (from $20,000 up to $250,000), sometimes in terms of separate illnesses. A $10,000 or $20,000 lifetime limit is tissue-thin protection indeed, while a $20,000 limit per illness might be barely tolerable. Best of all, of course, is a policy with no maximum limits.

There are two other things to look for. Make sure the policy is guaranteed renewable to at least age 65, a vital piece of protection that keeps the company from canceling you out, or raising your premiums unilaterally just because you've had the misfortune to have filed a number of claims.

Also check the policy for exclusions (no reimbursement for mental illness, for example), and the waiting period on "pre-existing" conditions. Many policies will pay off on the recurrence of an old illness, but only if you've not been under treatment for at least 90 days. In some cases, the exclusionary period runs for a year.

Many carriers have traditionally restricted their coverage on mental illness. They argue treatment is usually so prolonged and so uncertain that the risk could not be prudently taken on. The advent of psychotropic drugs and other advances in psychiatric treatment, however, has whittled down whatever validity the argument ever had. There are at least 20 states—more are on the way—where insurers are now required to make coverage for mental illness on at least an optional basis. In many cases, though, the coverage won't be volunteered. You have to ask for it, and pay extra for it.

Much of what we've said about major medical insurance applies to disability income protection. The length of the waiting period before payment begins is, in effect, a deductible that has much to do with your costs. There is a co-insurance factor, too. Disability policies pay off on only a portion of what you were grossing when you bought the policy—generally no more than two-thirds of what you were making.

Like major medical, disability insurance can be difficult to buy on an individual basis, particularly if you work at home or are self-employed. And like major medical, you have to look at benefit periods and exclusions with a hawk eye. Some policies will cover any one disability for no more than a year. Others will provide coverage up to age 65, or even life. Some policies define disability very narrowly. They pay off only if you can't "engage in any occupation for remuneration or hire." Other less restrictive policies stipulate only that you must be unable to work at your "regular occupation."

There is a world of difference between those definitions. Under the most stringent, a football coach permanently benched by chronic cardiac problems might not be entitled to disability benefits because he's capable of engaging in some other occupation— running the projection machine, for example.

The fine print really has to be scrutinized for distinctions of that kind. As with major medical coverage, you also have to make sure that the disability policy cannot be canceled just because you have become what is known in the trade as an "impaired risk."

Check out the renewal provisions, too. Coverage renewable "at the option of the company" may leave you with no options at all. Coverage described as "guaranteed renewable" may mean that rates can be lifted to prohibitive levels every time the policy comes due. The best form of coverage is "guaranteed renewable" and "noncancelable"—a combination that makes for level premiums for as long as you choose to hold on to the policy.

Both of those features can generally be found on the disability riders attached to life insurance policies. Usually, though, the amount of coverage available under such riders is itself limited—$10 a month for each $1,000 worth of life insurance bought is a common arrangement. The narrowness of those limits is one of the reasons why it makes sense to buy disability separately rather than as part of a package.

TOP DOLLAR TIPS

(1) Keep your medical and disability insurance premiums low by accepting the biggest deductible you can afford.

(2) You can also cut costs by electing longer waiting periods and settling for less generous co-insurance clauses.

(3) Blue Cross/Blue Shield policies are all right as far as they go, but most don't go far enough. They need to be beefed up with major medical protection.

(4) If your employer doesn't provide major medical on a group basis, try to put your own group together. If that doesn't work, maybe you can get low cost group coverage through an ethnic or fraternal organization.

HOW TO MAKE MONEY IN REAL ESTATE

Chapter 9

Finding the Home You Want

If you're on the lookout for one of the world's best investments, you may—if you're lucky—not have to search any further than the walls around you. Over the last decade, your average run-of-the-mill one-family house has proved to be a better inflation hedge than U.S. Government bonds, Treasury bills, common stocks and just about anything else you'd care to mention.

Fueled by heavy demand, and a supply that just never seems to catch up with the deep-rooted desire for a place of one's own, housing costs are out of sight. Increases of 12 percent a year (and in some parts of the country even more) have not been uncommon. Listen to Eugene F. Fama and G. William Schwert, who teach finance at the University of Chicago's Graduate School of Business and the University of Rochester's Graduate School of Management, respectively.

In a study put together with regression analysis and other tools of the number cruncher's trade, the two men concluded that "only private residential real estate" has proved to be "a complete hedge . . . against inflation."

One doesn't have to be a dedicated reader of the highly technical *Journal of Financial Economics*, which is where the Fama-Schwert study was first published, to realize that something extraordinary has been going on in housing. Most homeowners have been in a position to get their money back—and then some—almost anytime they wanted to sell.

The trend has been so strong that there has been quite a lot of speculative trading in houses, almost as though they were so many hot stocks. That doesn't necessarily mean, however, that some people haven't lost money on a turnaround, or that the trend is going to continue forever. The upsurge, however, is something that you should very definitely take into account if you're trying to decide whether you're better off buying a house or renting.

At bottom, the answer to that question has to be a personal one. It cannot be framed totally in terms of numbers or investment opportunities. Some people are apartment dwellers because they don't like to grapple with the sticky storm windows and persnickety plumbing that are the ultimate lot of most homeowners. Many people prefer the flexibility of apartment living. If the landlord proves to be unspeakable, one can always pick up and move on.

There is a certain amount of financial flexibility to renting, too. Instead of sinking, say, $6,000 into a down payment, insurance premiums and closing costs on a $50,000 house, a confirmed renter might prefer to put his spare cash into something conservative like Governments, or even a savings account. At 6 percent, the nest egg would double in a dozen years. The renter, based on past performance, wouldn't be as far ahead as the homeowner, but he would not have done all that badly.

The one big difference, of course, is that much of the growth in the homeowner's equity would have been tax-sheltered. The interest payments on the mortgage are tax deductible, and so are real estate tax payments. Those are out-of-pocket expenses that the renter pays at least indirectly through his monthly rent check, of course, without getting the same benefits as the homeowner. The higher your tax bracket is, the more useful those deductions become.

Take an example worked out by the Bank of America executive financial counseling service—a $100,000 house bought with a 20 percent down payment and financed with a 30-year 9.25 percent mortgage. The mortgage interest payments ($7,378 a year) and real estate taxes ($2,400) amount to a total of $9,778. The after-tax cost of those items to someone in the 60 percent bracket would be $3,911 a year. Throw in insurance and mortgage principal payments of $1,022 and you've got a total after-tax cost, not including maintenance expenses, of $4,933. That's a per month rental equivalent of $411. "What this example points out," the bank's executive financial counselors contend, "is that in a typical market it is cheaper to buy than rent, since you cannot rent a $100,000 residence for $411 a month."

Analytically, the example is a bit skimpy. It doesn't go into such niceties as the forgone "opportunity cost" of the cash that went into the down payment. The example reinforces the highly valid point, though, that tax savings make owning a house, a condominium, or a co-operative apartment significantly cheaper over the long haul than renting. The longer you own, the better comparison becomes, at least on the basis of the last quarter-century or so, because of the equity build-up.

For short periods, though—three to five years, maybe—the expense of buying and selling a house (closing costs, real estate commissions and the like) can put a very deep hole in even the most inflated resale values. Thus, the new class of migrant workers—corporate types who get moved around a lot—may be better off renting rather than buying.

Some other situations in which it might be better to rent than buy:

● When you want to settle into a community and learn more about it before making any deeper commitment.

● When you're not sure salary increases will come along fast enough to enable you to afford as much house as you would like to buy.

● When you're not sure where you want to live, or

when your family plans haven't gelled sufficiently for you to determine how much house you will need.

Whether you're renting or buying, there are certain determinations you will have to make about where you want to live. One key factor in that determination is how far you're willing to commute to work. Circle what seems to be a supportable area on the map, and work your way through the neighborhoods or towns that you've circumscribed. Do you plan to drive, or travel by public transportation? Check out the travel time under rush hour conditions. Talk to as many people as you can. Is the rail or bus service reliable? How much will it cost?

Here are some other items that should go on the house hunter's checklist:

• What is the quality of such public services as police and fire protection, and garbage pick-up? Is there a hospital within comparatively easy reach? Find out from the town clerk how quickly taxes and assessments have been rising in comparison with neighboring communities. Is the town (or subdivision) relatively undeveloped? If so, the cost of the infrastructure—roads and schools, for example— will almost certainly mean much higher taxes to come.

• Keep a weather eye peeled for such less than congenial neighbors as airports, chemical plants, refineries and superhighways. Their traffic patterns and aromas may make life miserable for you and at the same time detract from the resale value of your house.

• What is the quality of the schools and how far

away are they? Quiz the principal and the chairman of the board of education as to how well the schools are doing on state-administered achievement tests in the 3 Rs. What percentage of the high school graduating class goes on to college, and what sort of colleges do they get accepted at?

● How tough are the zoning laws and how rigidly are they enforced? Will some industrial or commercial developer be able to flip your neighborhood into a shopping mall or a cluster of warehouses? Is the local golf course a vacuum likely to be filled with cluster housing that will mess up the town's density?

Central to your study of the environment is an inventory of your own likes and needs. What do you want to see in a house? Are you Julia Childs and the "Galloping Gourmet" rolled into one? That sounds like a big kitchen with a lot of elbow room. Do you do a lot of formal entertaining? That sounds like more dining room than a breakfast nook can provide. There are always trade-offs on such things, and one has to be prepared to make them. Draw up a three-way list of items that are essential, merely desirable, and optional.

Such list making sometimes borders on fantasy and sometimes on the obsessional as well, but anything that sharpens your sense of what you're looking for is all to the good. Unless you're part of the intrepid "brownstone" movement that has sprung up in many of the nation's big cities—urban pioneers who hope to buy cheaply and renovate in poor neighborhoods that seem to be on the upswing—focus on the most expensive area you can afford. From an investment point of view, and perhaps for more esthetic reasons as well, it's the smart thing to do.

Within that neighborhood, though, note the Bank of America's financial counselors, "you should choose not the most expensive house, but a moderate to lower-priced house." "This type of house," the counselors continue, "stands a much better chance of appreciating without outstripping the market and becoming the most expensive house in the neighborhood."

Most house hunters, particularly corporate employees who may have to sell within a couple of years when they get shipped off to a new post, tend to be conservative in their choices.

"A house which is unique as to either price, design and floor plan, or location, will normally not appreciate as quickly as a house which is standard for an area," insist the B of A financial wizards. "The unique house will normally sell at your asking price only to that small percentage of buyers who are also interested in its unique qualities."

In general, that means shying away from 1787 stone houses that have only one bath, or tiny doll houses tucked away in huge lots. The trick is to buy a house that lends itself to traditional financing. As the Bank of America notes, "This may not be the house of your dreams, but it does protect you from taking a loss. Remember that selling the house for what you paid for it after two years probably means that you lost money in our inflationary economy."

You don't want to buy a pig in a poke. What you

want is a healthy house. Leave the deep diagnostic stuff to the experts, but here are some early warning symptoms to be on the alert for:

1.   Are there signs of dampness in the basement, or water damage in the ceilings?

2.   Is the paint peeling or blistering?

3.   Is the roof sagging in what may be a sign of rafter decay?

4.   Is the plumbing leaky? Is there adequate water pressure?

5.   Do doors sag or windows stick?

6.   Uneven floors? Are there spots that feel spongy when you walk on them?

7.   Is the caulking around windows, doors and joints crumbling and dried out?

8.   What about the caulking around tubs, sinks and shower?

9.   Are the gutters and downspouts leaking?

10.   Does water drain towards the house?

Clem Labine, editor of the *Old-House Journal* (199 Berkeley Place, Brooklyn, N.Y. 11217), and a respected brownstone renovator himself, suggests that home hunters interested in doing some preliminary inspection work on their own would do well to carry a tool kit with them. It includes a flashlight (for checking out water stains in dark basement corners); a marble (for checking the pitch of floors); a pair of binoculars (for a closer view of shingles and cornices); and an ice pick (to probe for termites).

The preliminary probe is likely to raise questions best answered by a professional. Many realtors maintain that no one should buy any kind of house—new or used—without having the structure examined by an expert. Others contend the diagnostic treatment really isn't necessary with the average new suburban house, but consider a survey a must with older houses.

The expert can be a professional engineer, or a professional inspector of lesser pedigree. Neither is to be confused with an appraiser, whose job it is to put a value on the house. John J. Roswell, a professional engineer who has been in the home inspection business in the New York metropolitan area since 1967, explains the difference. "Our function is really a diagnostic one," he says. "We like to think we can save people from making mistakes."

The business draws on many of the engineering disciplines—a knowledge of stress and materials, for instance—but there are many competent inspectors around who don't have a P.E. after their name. Where to find them? Generally by word of mouth from satisfied customers, through realtors, or through lawyers who specialize in real estate.

Talk to a couple of inspectors. Ask them for samples of the reports they've done for other people. All such reports should include a check of walls and foundations for structural problems; a test of the plumbing, heating and electrical systems; a survey of roofs and ceilings for possible leaks; cellars for water, and beams for termites. The report should be comprehensive enough to give the prospective buyer some insight into what it would cost to remedy any defects that have been turned up.

The dollar figures are important because they can often give the buyer enough leverage to bargain down the price of the house by at least the cost of the repairs. In some cases, in fact, a report might unearth enough serious problems to warn a buyer off entirely.

Inspection costs vary, so as always, it pays to shop. Some inspectors peg their costs to the size of the building surveyed, others partly to its sales value. All such inspections should be completed before you sign a contract to buy. Make sure, too, that the inspector's responsibility runs directly to you and to no one else, such as a contractor or a real estate agent. An inspector carrying water on both shoulders can put you at the mercy of a conflict of interests.

TOP DOLLAR TIPS

(1)   If you're renting, maybe you'd better think again. Owning a home has proved to be a complete hedge against inflation—and then some.

(2)   Not everyone should buy, though. If you get moved around a lot on your job, renting may be a smarter alternative.

(3)   Where you want to live often depends on the answer to one other key question. How far are you willing to commute to work?

(4)   Buy in the best neighborhood you can afford, but don't buy the most expensive or most unusual house in the neighborhood.

Chapter 10

FINANCING
A HOME

Like most runaway bull markets, the housing market is shot through with paradoxes and excesses. Perversely enough, one of the very features that has made the one-family residence such an attractive buy—sharply rising prices—has put buying a home out of reach for many middle-income people.

The unhappy fact is that housing prices have been rising much faster than income. Throw in the equally inconvenient fact that inflation has given wings to the cost of maintaining a house—real estate taxes, interest charges, heating bills—and you've got an equation that comes out unbalanced against young married couples particularly.

Census Bureau figures indicate that it costs a minimum of about $450 a month to cover the mortgage payments, property taxes and utility costs on a new home in the $45,000 to $50,000 bracket. That's a lot of bread, even for a two-paycheck family. Taking the standard rule of thumb—a 20 percent down payment, monthly carrying charges equal to no more than a week's salary—it's easy to understand why many young people despair of ever being able to afford a house.

The despair is there. New York's Citibank, for example, recently did a survey in which one out of every three people interviewed said they'd put off buying a home because they didn't have enough money for a down payment. Disenchantment is so wide-spread that the United States League of Savings Associations commissioned a sampling of 8,500 mortgage borrowers at nearly 200 savings associations across the country. The League hoped to dispel the "myth" that home buyers must be "middle aged and wealthy."

Take another look at your spending habits. Include everything—clothing, entertainment, food—but do not take into account rent, utilities and whatever you might have laid out for such household maintenance items as painting, papering, or redecorating.

Filtering out all of your expenses except direct household costs from income will give you two important figures: the amount of cash you can put into carrying a house, and a sense of some of the things you could give up if you want to stretch a bit in buying a house.

"Stretching" is very much part of the scene these

days; so much so, in fact, that many bankers are willing to bend the old 20 percent down—no more-than-a-week's-salary-carrying-charges rule of thumb for upward mobile young people whose prospects appear to be good. A certain amount of caution is necessary, but on the whole it pays to stretch as much as you can. Housing prices have been moving so fast that the home you can barely touch this year is likely to be completely out of reach next year.

For openers, it's smart to have a banking relationship. When you open the savings account you hope will ultimately materialize into your down payment, introduce yourself to a bank officer. Chat a bit about your aims and the institution's lending policies. If you don't like what you hear, take your money elsewhere.

Most lenders are willing to offer somewhat better terms to individuals who have been on the books for a while than to walk-ins. "For a depositor who's been with us for a while, we'll bend over backwards," says a lending officer at a major New York City savings bank. "For someone who just walks in the door and hasn't been a depositor, we're likely to be a lot tougher."

A secretary in a New York law firm and her husband, for example, recently floated on a cloud of delight out of a savings bank where they'd been clients for a little over three years with a really good deal: an 8.25 percent loan mortgage and a 13 percent down payment. At the time, less favored borrowers were being asked to pay 8.5 percent and put a full 20 percent down.

From the point of view of investment strategy,

you're better off buying the most house you can with the lowest down payment you can negotiate. That strategy holds, though, only if you are thinking in terms of what financial types call "leverage." If you buy a $100,000 house with a $20,000 down payment and subsequently resell it for $125,000 you've got a gross profit of 125 percent ($25,000 ÷ $20,000) on your money. If you buy and sell at the same prices on a down payment of only $10,000, the gross return works out to 250 percent on the cash investment.

Leverage is a nice thing to have going for you on the upside, but low down payments translate into proportionately higher monthly carrying charges. Make sure you can handle them before committing yourself. If your salary increases are reasonably predictable and you can persuade a banker that you're on the fast track, why not reach? It's done all the time.

"There are times when we will stretch," says Leonard Saltzman, a vice-president of the West Side Federal Savings and Loan Association in Manhattan, "if we are dealing with someone who is relatively young and whose employer has indicated that prospects for continued employment and advancement are good." The moral is clear: get your employer's character reference into the act and try to use whatever connections you can at the bank where your company does business.

The lowest down payments of all are to be found on Government-guaranteed mortgages. Veterans Administration guaranteed loans, in fact, usually require no down payment at all, and carry a low interest rate of 8 percent. Mortgages guaranteed by the Federal Housing Administration also carry an 8 percent rate (plus ½ of 1 percent for insurance). The maximum down payment is $3,750 on a maximum loan of $45,000.

Government guaranteed loans are often subject to a one-time charge of 1 percent (a "point" in banker's argot), payable at the closing. The premium is designed to give lenders some compensation for the higher rate they might be able to get on "conventional" or standard home loans. The premium is also supposed to compensate for the red tape that many bankers complain they have to endure in processing Government-backed mortgages. Many banks simply will not handle either V.A. or F.H.A. loans. Those that do, shoot for economies of scale by taking on large numbers of the Government-backed loans. Such loans are rarely advertised. Finding a banker who deals in V.A. and F.H.A. paper generally requires leg work.

The industry's dissatisfaction with the Government programs has opened a vast new market for private mortgage insurance (P.M.I.) pioneered by the MGIC Investment Corp. and now sold through lenders by about a dozen other companies. P.M.I. does not protect the homeowner. It protects the lender by insuring against default the difference between the down payment you make (often as low as 5 percent) and the down payment the banker would ordinarily ask you to make (often as much as 20 percent).

P.M.I., because it encourages lenders to grant mortgages on thinner equities than they otherwise would, is particularly valuable for young people who have a hard time getting enough cash together. The costs are pretty much standard. The first-year premium is usually ½ of 1 percent of the unpaid balance of the mortgage—$250 on a $50,000 loan, for example. Thereafter the cost falls to ¼ of 1 percent until the coverage can be dropped. That usually happens when the loan is amortized to 75 percent of the purchase price of the house. Few owners with that much of an equity in a house ever default on a loan. It's a fork in the statistical road at which bankers begin to breathe a bit more easily and is generally reached about seven years out in the life of the loan. With most of the risk out of the deal, there is no longer any need to carry the coverage.

Many bankers argue that the P.M.I. is more flexible than F.H.A. insurance. "You pay for it only as long as you need it and not for the full term of the mortgage, the way you do with an F.H.A. guarantee," says Robert Straussheim, a senior official of the Marine Midland Bank in New York. The effect of the insurance is to add another ¼ percent to your interest charges, but most borrowers apparently feel the trade-off is a useful one.

Though it's been around for 20 years, P.M.I. is clearly a tool whose time has come. Circumstances have a way of forging new instruments and P.M.I. is just one of several aimed at easing some of the financial burden that rising prices and interest rates have placed on homebuyers.

The graduated mortgage payment plan (G.M.P.), for example, is slowly evolving into a vehicle that could have a marked impact on the ability of people in the $14,000 to $25,000 a year bracket to buy a home. As the name suggests, the payments on G.M.P. loans start at a lower than normal level and then gradually increase to a higher than normal level—presumably in step with increases in the homeowner's income.

G.M.P.s and their "life cycle" approach to earning power got a rather lukewarm reception from bankers at first. Frankly an experiment, they were sponsored by the U.S. Department of Housing and Urban Development and applied only to F.H.A. mortgages. Given the bankers' reluctance to underwrite Government-backed loans at 8.25 percent during a period when conventional mortgages were yielding 9 percent or better, G.M.P.'s were slow to get off the ground.

Growing discontent with the rigidities of a financing package that has not changed in 40 years, however, is percolating through the industry. Bankers realize there is a need for innovation and there has been a gingerly move to conventional G.M.P.s.

The Community State Bank of Albany started the ball rolling in New York with a plan that worked like this: Ordinarily the carrying costs on a standard 25-year mortgage carrying an interest rate of 8.5 percent would run to an unvarying $241.56 a month. A homebuyer would have to be making at least that much money a week to qualify for the loan. Restructured as a G.M.P., the carrying charges were pegged at $215.62 in the first year, gradually increased to $228.11 in the fifth year, and in later years leveled off at $255.50 a month.

The later payments, of course, make up for the comparatively modest size of the earlier ones. Though the homebuyer winds up paying more interest dollars over the life of a G.M.P. than with a conventional loan, many bankers are concerned about the slow pay down of the principal on the mortgage—a concern that explains some of their reluctance to move with the new wave.

There has been somewhat broader acceptance of a variation on the G.M.P., the so-called FLIP mortgages, an acronym for Flexible Loan Insurance Program. Designed by the FLIP Mortgage Corporation of Newtown, Pa., and marketed to lenders by purveyors of private mortgage insurance, the FLIPs are tailored to meet bankers' objections to the slow equity build-up in G.M.P.s.

They do so by putting the bulk of the buyer's down payment in a pledged escrow account with the lender. In most cases, the down payment is only 5 percent because of the private mortgage insurance link. The early payments are scaled low, as with any G.M.P., but are supplemented during the first five years of the loan by the principal and interest that the lender draws on a regularly scheduled basis from the escrow account.

How does the FLIP work in real life? Allan Smith, head of FLIP Mortgage, gives the example of a person who earns $13,500 a year and can reasonably expect salary increases of about 5.5 percent a year. At that salary level, assuming a $3,500 down payment on a 30-year 9 percent loan, a FLIP-backed buyer would be able to purchase a house worth $37,500. Paying that much with a conventional mortgage would require a salary of $16,500 a year.

Much of the experimentation with new mortgage forms has focused on incentives to keep bankers in the mortgage market during periods of rising interest costs when their earnings are being squeezed. The interest charge on variable rate mortgages, for example, fluctuates with the cost of money generally. There are clear advantages on the banker's side, of course, but some trade-offs for the homeowner, too. The latter has the option of extending his mortgage at the old rate instead of electing to absorb a higher one. Further, the basic rate on V.R.M.s generally runs ¼ point lower than on conventional loans. V.R.M.s are common in California, but they have been aggressively pushed by some New England banks, too.

Are you better off with a fixed rate rather than a variable rate loan? If interest rates in general are low, why not lock your own costs in at a fixed rate? If interest rates are very high, conventional rates rise too. When that happens, there might be some virtue in going the variable route on the assumption that basic rates might soon be going down.

One area in which it pays to make no assumptions are the closing costs that go with the purchase of a home. They include loan origination fees, a title search, title insurance, mortgage insurance, advance payments on real estate taxes and a host of other niggling items that can very quickly add up to 5 percent or more of your down payment.

Some of the costs—a title search and title insurance, for example—are a costly heritage of an archaic property record-keeping system that dates to Colonial times. It's nice to be able to take a detached historical view, but there are times when perspective does not help. Between down payments, new rugs and furniture and the like, most people are feeling a bit strapped when they buy a home. A couple of thousand dollars worth of closing costs adds to the sense of financial distress. The important thing to remember is that some closing costs are not graven in stone. They are often negotiable and as susceptible as anything else to informed shopping.

Start off by reading "Settlement Costs," a booklet put out by H.U.D. It explains your rights and can be got through most lenders, or by writing the Superintendent of Documents, U.S. Government Printing Office, Washington D.C. 20402.

As the booklet explains, the lender is required to give you a "good faith" estimate of most of the settlement costs you'll be asked to meet.

Here is a breakdown of the closing costs on a $50,000 house that recently changed hands in Rutherford, N.J. The list is not atypical:

One-year premium, homeowner's, fire, theft, and liability insurance	$275
Legal fees and title search	675
Bank's Lawyer	100
Title Insurance	268
Mortgage Insurance	918
Quarterly real-estate taxes	292
Bank Charge for Mortgage Filing	100
Property Survey	125
Deed and Mortgage	25
Total	$2,778

There might be other items on the list—an appraisal fee, for example, or accrued interest running from the date of the settlement to the beginning of the period covered by the first monthly payment.

In the example at hand there was no give at all in such items as the quarterly tax payment and the mortgage recording fees. A bit of comparison shopping also quickly established that nothing much could be done with the mortgage insurance premium that amounted to almost one-third of the entire closing bill. Calls to three major purveyors of P.M.I. elicited no difference in rates. The companies like to think of themselves as competing in terms of service rather than price.

There is, however, fairly tough competition between direct sellers of homeowner's insurance and those who sell through agents. The purchaser got a quote of $140 from All State Insurance, but decided in the end to throw the business (at an additional cost of $135) to an agent—an old family friend who could be counted on to provide first-rate service.

The $275 charge by the purchaser's lawyer was the best that could be found. He, too, was an old family friend and was willing to work more cheaply—he even helped in the search for mortgage money—than five other lawyers the purchaser asked to bid on the job. The purchaser says he could have saved "$15 or $25" with some of the other title insurance companies he checked out, but in the end decided to go along with the one suggested by his lawyer.

Paying the bank's lawyer to read the same documents that his own lawyer had checked seemed a bit much to the buyer. So did the need to pay for both a title search and title insurance on a house that had changed hands only twice in the 45 years of its existence. But there was one consolation. The purchaser knew he had shopped intelligently. He had done the best he could for the best reasons he could find, and you can't do any better than that.

TOP DOLLAR TIPS

(1)   Stretch to buy as much house as you can. The house you can barely touch this year is likely to be completely out of reach next year.

(2)   A little leverage—business references, for example—can help get you a better mortgage deal.

(3)   With the help of private mortgage insurance, you might be able to get by with a down payment of as little as 5 percent.

(4)   If you can demonstrate that your earning power is going to grow, look into the possibility of getting a graduated mortgage—one on which the monthly payments start low and then expand as your income expands.

Chapter 11

GETTING CASH OUT OF YOUR HOUSE

There are maybe 55 million one- and two-family homes in the U.S. in which their owners have an equity of $1.5 trillion, according to a recent estimate by *Forbes* magazine. Expressed another way, that is $1,500 billion. Or, for a better grasp of the enormity of the figure, try $1,500,000,000,000.

That's a lot of capital to have tied up in bricks and mortar, a realization that has suddenly penetrated the consciousness of a lot of Americans. It's money in the bank. At last report, homeowners were digging into that equity through some form of refinancing at the rate of more than $16 billion a year. The cash poured into home improvements, second homes, college educations, boats, automobiles, vacations and the hundreds of other goodies that make up the Great American Shopping List.

There are several ways to pry the lid off the jam, a confection that consists mainly of endlessly rising prices. One approach is to refinance the entire mortgage—in effect, take out an entirely new loan. Another is to get a second mortgage on the difference between the unpaid balance of the original loan and 75 percent to 80 percent of the new market value of the house. The objective in both cases, of course, is to capture and put to work in other ways at least part of the value that has been accumulating tax-free in the house.

Take the case of the Meriden, Conn., couple who bought a bungalow four years ago for $48,000 with the help of a $40,000 mortgage at 8 percent. By last year the market value of the house had climbed to around $65,000. On the basis of the new value, the couple was able to get a new mortgage of $48,000. After paying off the balance of the old loan, and a new—if somewhat abbreviated—set of closing costs the couple came away with about $10,000 net. The cash went right back into the house in the form of two new bedrooms and a bath that will help accommodate a growing family.

The closing costs—about $700 worth of attorney's fees, appraisal fees and new title insurance—have to be figured as part of the cost of liberating the capital build-up in the house. Interest rates had been rising, too, and so the new loan went on the books at 8.25

percent. The result was an increase of about $40 in new monthly carrying charges.

The examples are endless: The New York City public relations man, for instance, who had put $50,000 cash into a $90,000 two-family home he built on Staten Island. The area is booming. Three years after the housewarming, the structure was worth more than $115,000. A refinancing netted Bob Williams, the public relations man, about $20,000. Some of that went to pay off an accumulation of bills ("I'd been putting most of my spare cash back into the house," says Mr. Williams), the balance into a cash reserve. Mr. Williams' monthly carrying charge took a pretty big jump, but his income has gone up since he built the house, and he figures he can handle the additional load without any trouble.

Higher monthly carrying charges can be a rub. Anyone who has held on to a house for any length of time is almost invariably going to be faced with the prospect of higher interest rates. Tax deductions help to reduce some of the sting, but they are by no means the compleat poultice. For older people approaching retirement, or others whose income is likely to decline, refinancing may not be the best play in the world—however attractive the prospect of having a big chunk of capital in hand.

There's no point in investing the capital elsewhere unless you're sure you can get a better after-tax return than the new rate you're paying to the bank. And, unhappily, borrowed money cannot be reinvested in tax-exempt securities. One of the best places to reinvest the proceeds of a refinancing might be in another house—a summer home, for example, that you might rent out part-time.

Some banks are more conservative than others, but in general most will lend up to 70 percent to 80 percent of the new market value of a house in a straight refinancing for a term that might stretch for as long as 25 years. The loan-to-value ratio is sometimes the same with second mortgages, but the latter invariably carry higher interest rates (10 percent to 13 percent is typical), and shorter maturities (typically 10 to 15 years).

Say your home is worth $80,000 and the balance on the first mortgage is $45,000. A second mortgage lender might advance as much as 77 percent of the difference between the two values, or about $27,000. Often, though, the lenders will not go that far. Many set limits of $15,000 to $20,000, and the typical loan is more likely to be in the $5,000 to $10,000 range. The cost is not cheap. Borrow $10,000 for 10 years at 12 percent, and your carrying charges will come to just under $145 a month. On the whole, second mortgages probably work better than straight refinancings for borrowers who want to work down their loans fairly quickly and are willing to pay extra for the privilege. Because of the high interest rates to bear, second mortgages are not the best way to finance home improvements.

If adding a new porch or finishing a basement is what you have in mind, one of your best bets is either an F.H.A. guaranteed or "conventional" home improvement loan. The rates aren't always all that much lower in comparison with second mortgages, but there are no new layers of closing costs to grapple with. With an F.H.A. loan, you can borrow up to $7,500 at most banks and up to $10,000 at some mutual institutions for as long as 10 years at an annual interest rate of 12 percent. The one proviso is that the improvement be permanent and part of the house. Thus, garages and playrooms qualify for F.H.A. money, but swimming pools do not.

The limits and rates on conventional home improvements vary from bank to bank and state to state. Long term rates (from one to 10 years) range from around 11.5 percent to about 13.5 percent. The best deals can often be had on short term loans (a year to a year and a half), where you can frequently dicker at rates ranging from around 9.5 percent to a little over 11 percent, depending on what's happening in the money markets generally.

Three other even lower cost potential sources of home improvement money, as you'll remember from Chapter 4, are securities, passbook, and life insurance loans. Not all improvements add dollar-for-dollar to the value of your house. Some—a new heating system, for example—might not do much more than keep you competitive with your neighbors. If you're about to put your house up for sale, however, some cosmetic surgery may be in order. Selling, after all, is another way of capitalizing on what may be the biggest chunk of equity you have working for you. You don't want to underprice yourself, but neither do you want to price yourself out of the market.

One way to position yourself is to get the house

appraised. Another is to check out the tax assessor on the prices at which similar houses in the neighborhood have been going for. With the way housing prices have appreciated, selling out—depending on whether you plan to buy another home or not—can have serious tax implications.

At age 55 you are entitled to a one-time tax exclusion of up to $100,000 on the profit you make on a house, but you must have owned and lived in the place for three of the preceding five years. That's a nice break for individuals getting ready to slip into a retirement program that includes a move to a warmer climate; or for "empty nesters" planning to flee from the old homestead into something smaller, like an apartment. The tax break can be substantial. If you're thinking of such a move and you're in your early 50s, consider the possibility of putting off the change until you (or your spouse) reach the magic age of 55.

Below age 55, you are liable to the capital gains levy only if you don't buy another house within 18 months, and even then only if the new house costs less than the price tag on the one you sold. If you don't buy another home within the 18 month time frame, the standard capital gains levy comes into play on your profit.

One way to beat the tax bite, and generate some partly tax-free income as well, is to take back a purchase money mortgage from the buyer. Consider the case of a woman we'll call Margaret, a Greenwich, Conn., widow whose children had long since grown, and who had become increasingly irritated with "house sitting." Her four bedroom home had a market value of $67,500. The house had been appraised for estate purposes at $20,000. Margaret consequently faced the joyless prospect of paying a capital gains tax on her $47,500 profit.

There was one potential off-set. Margaret had thought about investing some of the proceeds in a condominium. To the extent she did so, Margaret would have reduced the amount of her profit subject to tax dollar-for-dollar. Closer inspection of the condos she could afford, however, convinced Margaret she would be better off renting. That decision slammed the door on tax shelter, since Margaret still had a couple of years or so before she could take advantage of the age 55 tax-free "rollover."

As it turned out, Margaret was able to get a bit more for her house than she expected—$69,000 or $1,500 over the market value. After consultation with her lawyer and accountant, Margaret decided to help a carefully screened buyer finance the house.

She took a $17,000 down payment, and the balance of the cash in a 25-year mortgage at 8.5 percent—about as good as the then going rate on top-ranked corporate bonds. The nice thing about the yield is the tax shelter it offers. Because she was careful not to take a down payment of more than 30 percent, Margaret qualified for a special section of the tax code. It permits her to spread the profit on the sale of the house over the life of the mortgage at low capital gains rates. Most of the $418 in mortgage payments she receives every month is taxed as ordinary income because it is interest income. Some $50 of the total, however, is partly a tax-free return of capital, and partly a capital gain taxed at preferential rates. The amount of money sheltered will increase as the mortgage approaches maturity.

The tax bill would have been even smaller if Margaret had been willing to take a lower down payment, but insisting on the substantial up-front payment of $17,000 was part of her strategy. A credit check of the buyer showed that he had an impeccable record, but her cautious lawyer and accountant convinced Margaret that almost any buyer would have a hard time "walking away from a down payment as big as $17,000."

Really sophisticated tax and legal advice is crucial in putting a purchase money mortgage deal together. Any such package should include a penalty clause on mortgage pre-payments that might upset your tax calculations, an iron-clad requirement that the buyer pay for the fire insurance that will protect the house, and rigid scrutiny of the buyer's ability to take the debt on.

TOP DOLLAR TIPS

(1) Think of your home as a source of locked in capital. What's the best way to get it out?

(2) A completely new mortgage can be a big help, but carries some disadvantages: another set of closing costs, and probably higher interest rate.

(3) For older people approaching retirement, or others whose income is likely to decline, refinancing is not a good idea.

(4) Thinking of selling? Why not get a good return and some tax advantages by taking the buyer's mortgage?

Chapter 12

CONDOS
AND CO-OPS

Tax advantages help to make the real estate mare go. Increasing awareness of those advantages, coupled with sweeping changes in life styles, have made condominiums and co-operative apartments all the rage. Late marriages, smaller families, the emergence of career women unwilling to trade good paying jobs for the traditional role of *hausfrau*, have all contributed to the sociological push into condos and co-ops. Why pay big rents when you can build equity and get the same tax advantages as homeowners—without doing all the donkey work of shoveling snow or pushing a lawn mower?

Why, indeed, is the answer. In many respects,

though, buying into a condo or co-op presents many more booby traps than buying a one- or two-family house. The commonality of ownership itself, if nothing else, often poses the very prickly problem of learning to live with one's fellows—and boards of directors. In a condo, you are the sole owner of the unit you occupy and a co-owner in such common spaces as the structure itself, stairs, hallways, and such recreational facilities as swimming pools and tennis courts. In a co-op, you hold a share in an organization that owns the entire structure and whatever property is attached to it.

Until fairly recently, it was a good deal more difficult to finance the purchase of a co-op than a condominium. In the case of a default, a lender had nothing to fall back on except a perhaps not too marketable share in a co-op where the board of directors held plenary power to decide to whom an apartment could or could not be sold. The line of control is clearer in a condo. There are still directors to deal with, but the collateral is a good deal more tangible—title to an apartment or a separate dwelling of some kind.

Thus, for a long time co-op buyers either had to be in a position to buy an apartment outright, or able to arrange financing outside regular commercial channels. All of that has begun to change now, and lenders have come up with all sorts of imaginative programs. The financing charges, of course, are separate from the pro-rata maintenance expenses it takes to pay the heat, light, tax and other operating bills.

Big city banks have been particularly active in the field. New York's Citibank, for example, not long ago even began marketing a kind of graduated mortgage plan for co-op buyers. The plan provides 85 percent financing on the first $40,000 of the purchase price and 40 percent financing on anything over that. In the first five years, the borrower would pay off only on the interest—$202 a month, on a $25,500 loan, for example. Thereafter the carrying charges would go to $237.70 a month and remain at that level for the life of the mortgage.

With a condo, of course, you can write off your own mortgage interest payments and your share of the real estate taxes. In a co-op, you might get to write off anywhere from 40 percent to 70 percent of the monthly maintenance charges—your apartment's share of the mortgage on the building and real estate taxes.

Thus, on an after-tax basis, it's almost invariably cheaper to buy a condo or co-op than rent, even if you have to absorb some expenses like painting. The search process for a condo or co-op is really not much different from looking for a house. Among other things, you have to consider neighborhood, access to shopping and transportation, the condition of the property, and how well it has been maintained. In general, you are much better off buying into something that already exists rather than a bunch of roseate promises that have yet to make their way off the blueprints.

Many condos and co-ops are quarried out of older buildings that have been on the rental market for years. Opportunity or potential booby trap? It all depends. When you buy into a conversion, you take on not only an apartment, but the shell as well—stairways, the common walls, the wiring, the plumbing, and all the other ganglia that keep the place functioning. Are you buying a big dose of migraine? Only a really detailed engineering report can tell. Without such a report, done by an independent surveyor with solid credentials, you are flying blind. That's never a comfortable position to be in, especially when you're being asked to put a big bunch of money up front.

It's well to remember that money is a risk. One of the big difficulties with condos and co-ops is their market volatility. New York is not the world, but well situated, very modest one-family homes in Queens, for example, have been off in a little bull market all their own for years. Prices on stately co-ops at very posh addresses on Fifth Avenue and Park Avenue, on the other hand, have been bucketing all over the place. Great for people who bought at the lows; not too good for people who had to sell at them.

Market risks aside, there have been all kinds of promotional rip-offs. Condos have gone bust before completion, leaving hapless buyers scratching for deposits that somehow got sucked into the quagmire of the developer's business affairs. Too, maintenance costs have been low-balled—deliberately understated—to gull the unwary.

Hence, if you're in the market for a co-op or a condo, it pays to take a sharp look at the operating budget. Do so with a jaundiced eye. Maintenance costs have invariably gone only one way—up. Projecting just a bit, are you sure your personal budget has enough stretch to meet those costs?

Another sore spot to look for is what H.U.D. officials call "hidden leasehold costs." Some developers angle to keep control of part of a project—usually the recreation facilities—after turning the rest of the community over to condo buyers. The pitch generally is that allowing the developer to lease whatever he has kept will mean lower maintenance costs. What sometimes happens, of course, is that those costs suddenly skyrocket, leaving the condo owners with a Hobson's choice—pay the higher fees, or buy the developer out at an inflated price.

The moral is obvious: steer clear of deals that leave full control of leased property in the hands of someone else.

There are often pitfalls aplenty in the fine print of the master plan, the bylaws and the management agreement that bring the condo to life. Have a lawyer who is familiar with the condo (or co-op) form of ownership go through them with you carefully. Underlying all the fine print and the lawyering, of course, is the basic question of the developer's reputation and track record. What's his financial position? Has he ever put together a condo before? What do the owners there have to say about the way they've been treated? One useful reference is H.U.D.'s "Questions About Condominiums," a free 48-page booklet available on written request from the Consumer Information Center, Dept. 586E, Pueblo, Colo. 81009.

TOP DOLLAR TIPS

(1)   Bankers have loosened up a bit, but the purchase of a condo is often easier to finance than buying into a co-op.

(2)   Condo and co-op markets are far more volatile—and hence more risky—than the resale home market. There are times when it's a lot better to be a buyer than a seller.

(3)   If you're in the market for a condo or a co-op, don't let yourself be low-balled by low-ball maintenance estimates.

(4)   Look out for hidden leasehold costs.

Chapter 13

HOMEOWNER'S INSURANCE

Condo, co-op, or plain old traditional house—they all spell equity, equity that has to be protected. The standard way of doing so, of course, is to buy the package of fire, burglary, theft and liability coverage commonly known as homeowner's insurance. It's a must. Remember to keep your coverage in step with the rising value of your home. Not everyone does. "Forget about tax shelters and more complicated subjects like that," says Peter Mazonas, head of the Bank of America's executive financial counseling service. "The most common error of judgment I have found is that many executives just don't have enough fire insurance on their homes to compensate for the huge inflation in building costs."

Think of what inflation has done. A house that cost $15,000 to build a quarter-century ago would take $45,000 to replace today. A house that cost $25,000 ten years ago would take more than $50,000 to replace.

If you're in doubt about how much insurance you should be carrying, talk it over with your agent, or get a real estate appraiser to work out a figure for you. If tax assessments in your town are required to reflect full market value, that figure is probably good enough. Alternatively, you can get help from such independent insurance adjustment firms as GAB Business Services, Inc., of Princeton, N.J. Operating entirely by mail, GAB and other such services will send you a detailed work-sheet on the physical characteristics of your house to fill out. They'll put the numbers together, and for a very modest charge tell you how much coverage you should be carrying.

It's important to keep adding to your coverage at each renewal, if only to be certain that the protection you're carrying is equal to 80 percent of the replacement value of your home, not including land. The insurance company will pay off full replacement value only if you are at or above the 80 percent benchmark. If you slip below that ratio, the payoff will be on a depreciated basis.

The difference can be substantial. If you have a kitchen fire, for example, your cabinets and appliances may be eight years old, but so long as you're at the 80 percent ratio, the company will pay what it costs to put things together again at today's prices. If you're stuck with a depreciated settlement, however, the company might pay only half the replacement costs, leaving you to foot the balance.

Trying to keep up with inflation, though, can be costly. It's not so much that basic fire insurance rates have been rising so quickly as the need to keep adding additional coverage. In New York's Westchester County, for example, as in many metropolitan area suburbs, homeowner premiums as such have been climbing at about 6 percent a year. One Bronxville resident, however, was startled recently to discover that the total cost of his homeowner policy was up 29 percent this year and up more than 50 percent over the last two years. His experience was not unusual. Most of the increased cost had come from the increase in the value of his home.

One way to deal with the upsurge in costs is to take a higher deductible—the minimum amount of damage that has to be absorbed before the insurance company begins to pay off. Most homeowner policies carry a $100 deductible. There are some economies in going to a $250 or a $500 deductible—a premium credit of 10 percent up to a maximum of $30 and a premium credit of 20 percent up to a maximum of $60, respectively.

That's not much of a saving if you're laying out $540 a year to insure a $100,000 house. The best bet is to go to a $1,000 deductible, which carries a straight credit of 29 percent. It's a return to the basic insurance principle we talked about earlier—protect yourself against the big risks, let the little ones take care of themselves.

TOP DOLLAR TIPS

(1) *There's no way around it. Make sure to add enough to your fire insurance coverage every year to cover the inflation-fed increased value of your home.*

(2) *If you expect the insurance company to pay off on the basis of current values, be careful to keep the level of your coverage at 80 percent of the structure's replacement cost.*

(3) *Cut premium costs, up as much as 50 percent in some suburban areas, by going to a $1,000 deductible.*

Chapter 14

INVESTING
IN REAL ESTATE

The entrepreneurial itch, bless it, dies hard. Home ownership has proved to be such a good deal that many people have turned into part-time, do-it-yourself real-estate investors, and why not? There's ready capital to be had in refinancing the mortgage on the old homestead itself, and what better place to put it than another house—this time to rent out.

It's a nice fantasy to act out. Use one house to bootstrap another, the second to bootstrap a third, and so on and on. The income tax savings rise exponentially. Besides writing off real estate taxes and interest payments, with a rental unit going for you there are depreciation and maintenance costs to be taken, too.

Depreciation, actually a bookkeeping device, can be written off in several ways. The most common approach is to assume that the building has a useful life of 20 years. In each of those 20 years, you are entitled to deduct 5 percent of the value of the house.

Thus, a structure with a tax base of $50,000 would yield $2,500 in depreciation charges, which can be used to shelter rental or any other kind of income, including capital gains. And it doesn't have to be a single-family home, either. Two-family houses, which often enable the owner to live rent free while his equity builds, are probably one of the most widespread real estate ploys of all. But the same tax advantages attach to other multiple dwelling units, condominiums, and commercial property, too.

Residential property probably offers the novice somewhat more safety than commercial real estate. Stick to solid neighborhoods in which you know rental demand is high, and you are less likely to be exposed to swings in the business cycle that have played havoc with so many large scale commercial projects over the last several years.

Not that residential property carries any gilt-edged guarantees, either. Markets as far apart as Monmouth County, N.J., and Dade County, Fla., have only recently begun to recover from a glut of condominiums that were slapped together just in time to be swept by the chill winds of recession.

On paper, the tax write-offs and the high average rate of appreciation make real estate investment look like a good thing. But as a *rentier*, you have to think about the sweat equity involved, too. Unless you're dealing with large economies of scale that can be turned over to a professional manager, count it likely that you are at least going to have to keep close tabs on such killers of the dream as leaky faucets, leaky roofs and maybe leaky tenants, too. It helps to be handy. If you're not, maintenance costs—however tax deductible—are likely to eat you alive. Further, since most real estate investors continue to work full-time at other pursuits, you have to be sure that the sweat equity side of the business is a burden you're willing to take on.

Some resolve that problem by banding together in partnerships and dividing the labor. I know one such group that consists of a lawyer, an accountant, a stockbroker, and a construction worker. They started with one small four-apartment dwelling and now own fourteen others in suburban Bergen County, N.J., where good, moderately priced rentals are hard to come by.

The stockbroker does the selling, the construction man the maintenance, while the other two lend their legal and financial skills to the combine. It is a fairly hard-headed little group, playing for a combination of both tax-sheltered income that gets plowed back into the business and long term capital gains.

Many such investors feel that appreciation alone is the name of the game. Thus they are often willing to go along with what is known in the trade as a "negative cash flow"—a building that isn't paying its own way. There are tax offsets, of course, but going into a situation with the wide-eyed hope that a rising market will ultimately bail you out is asking for trouble.

As with any tax shelter, it's the basic earning power and not the gimmickry that counts.

One of the key investment rules is to stick to towns and neighborhoods that you know. A corollary is to stay away from towns that have rent control or rent leveling laws. What you're really investing in is a slice of the socio-economic pie. Thus, it also pays to stay away from one-industry towns. When appropriations for the space program began to fade like the Cheshire Cat, real estate values in such towns around the Cape Kennedy, Fla., launch center as Cocoa and Cocoa Beach began to fade right along with them. Equally, stay away from towns with a stable or declining tax base—a set of circumstances that almost invariably means higher real estate tax rates.

Costs are going to rise anyway, thanks to inflation, but there are practical limits as to how much of the impact can be passed on to tenants. Rents have been climbing just like everything else, of course, but they have not been climbing anything like housing prices. The widening gap between those two curves leaves the investor just that much less margin for error.

Hence, make sure that you do really solid research into what you're buying. Get all the fixed expenses for at least the last five years from the owner and rental income to match. A professional inspection report is an absolute must. What should you pay? That's all part of the negotiation. What are similar houses in the neighborhood going for? One rule of thumb is that a rental property ought to go for no more than eight times the annual rent roll, but that should be taken as no more than the roughest of guidelines.

What sort of a return can you anticipate? A more moderate one than you might expect, considering the personal effort that has to be put into managing real estate. Some investors consider themselves lucky to get a cash flow return of 7 percent on their money. That's not terribly exciting when you can get a tax-free yield of at least 5 percent in a passive investment like good quality municipal bonds.

Investing in developed real estate is not without risks, but compared with taking a flier in raw land it is a very conservative game indeed. Not that speculating in raw land doesn't have its rewards, too, but it's a crapshooter's game. The potential leverage is stunning because it is often possible to buy land for as little as 10 percent down, with the seller taking the mortgage. All you have to do is buy in the right place. *Vide* the old Texas joke: "So you're a rancher," said the Easterner to this grizzled old wrangler. "What's the name of your ranch?" "Oh, they call it downtown Dallas," came the reply.

If lightning in some form of population or industrial growth doesn't strike, it's easy to wind up in the soup. Land doesn't generate income. Except maybe for haying or logging revenues that might be enough to cover the taxes, land consumes income. There are mortgage payments to meet. Furthermore, land can be the most illiquid of investments. If you have to sell, there may not be anyone around willing to buy at any price, let alone what you're asking.

Land sales are big business—about $4 billion a year. A lot of land is sold on the never-never basis—

low down payments and small monthly carrying charges—by developers. "Watch the sunrise break over the valleys below from a mountaintop retreat," urges one advertisement.

Better to be the seller than the buyer, in most cases because many such promotions are just so much moose pasture. Many otherwise savvy types buy into such schemes without even first taking the elementary precaution of looking at what they're buying.

Maybe you can latch cheaply onto some land that will make a perfect rustic or seaside haven—land that will quickly escalate in value, too. But first, ask a few questions:

- Is the land the developer's to sell? Is his title clean? Any liens or mortgages on the lots?
- What about such basic utilities as water, sewerage and electricity? Are there soil or drainage problems? Is the water table so low that you won't be able to build on the land?

The answers to those questions, and many more, can be found in a reading of the "Statement of Record" many developers selling land interstate must file with H.U.D. Developers selling across state lines must also give potential buyers a "property report" that is an extract of the more detailed document filed with the government agency.

The basic document itself can be obtained from H.U.D.'s Office of Interstate Land Sales Registration, 451 7th Street, S.W., Washington, D.C. 20410. The cost is 25 cents a page, at this writing. Include the name of the developer, the development, and its location.

The statement of record is valuable because it contains, among other things, financial reports that should provide some inkling of whether the developer is solid enough to deliver on all the promises he is making.

The H.U.D. filing requirements, in fact, are a useful guide to the sort of information that should be dredged up before you buy almost any kind of property, developed or not. What about the availability of such facilities as schools, hospitals and transportation? How detailed are the plans for the property, including the construction of streets and recreational facilities?

Unfortunately, there are some loopholes in the disclosure rules. Only developers offering 50 or more unimproved lots interstate are bound by them. Subdivisions with lots of five acres or more are also exempt. The promotional patter tends to overlook the fact that land values are set by the complex interplay of location, supply, and demand.

They are variables that are difficult for even professionals to assess. In the meantime, the cost meter keeps running. The Urban Land Institute estimates that raw acreage must double in value every five years to justify hanging on to it as an investment. For more information, write the Consumer Information Center, Pueblo, Colo. 81009 for the H.U.D. brochure "Buying Lots from Developers." The 24-page booklet, at this writing, costs 50 cents.

TOP DOLLAR TIPS

(1) Thinking of making it big in real estate? Stick to residential properties. They're less risky than commercial properties.

(2) Maybe a partnership is the best way to handle part-time real estate investing. You share the wealth, but you share the labor, too.

(3) Concentrate on the basic earning power of a property. Don't expect a rising market to bail you out of a bad deal.

(4) There are big gains to be had in buying land, but there are plenty of risks, too.

HOW TO MANAGE YOUR INVESTMENTS

Chapter 15

SUCCESS IN THE STOCK MARKET

Common stocks may be as American as apple pie, but that doesn't mean you have to own any. For many people they are part of a balanced investment approach that includes a blend of Government bonds, short and long term, other fixed income securities, and maybe tax-exempt municipals, or some outright tax-shelter deals.

Common stocks are at the long end of the risk spectrum. If you like your risks short—if, in the argot of the Street, you "like to sleep nights"—then stay away from common stocks. There have been really only two periods when making money on Wall Street seemed to be as easy as shooting fish in a barrel—the 'twenties and part of the 'sixties. And both those periods ended in a *Götterdämmerung* of speculative flash from which few escaped.

Individuals, in fact, on balance have been sellers of common stock for years now, as if they felt equities had somehow been stamped injurious to their health. Stocks can be injurious to your health. If you've got a speculative turn of mind and can afford the risks, go to it. In fact, my own feeling is that if you are in stocks, at least part of your portfolio should contain a few carefully selected shoot-the-moon-type issues. But if you're short on cash reserves, or if your basic income is vulnerable to swings in the economy—sales, almost any kind of small business, for example—think twice about putting any cash at all in stocks. You might have to sell when you can least afford to. And after you've taken a look at the risk-reward ratios in the market as a whole, you might decide it makes much more sense to put your money to work elsewhere.

Listen to this. "There is a casino overtone. If you put your money in the stock market, there is a chance you won't get it all back. In fact, there is a fairly strong chance that you won't get it all back."

That is the considered judgment of Lawrence Fisher, professor of finance at the University of Chicago Graduate School of Business, and a man who knows perhaps better than any stockbroker just how hard it is to make money in the market.

Professor Fisher, along with James H. Lorie, also a member of the Chicago B-School faculty, is the author of the recently published *A Half Century of Returns on Stocks and Bonds.* The book, a computerized distillation of almost a million price changes, dividends and interest payments, was published by the B-School's Center for Research in Security Prices. The study was underwritten by Merrill Lynch, Pierce, Fenner & Smith, but the results could hardly have made the brokerage firm's thundering herd of salesmen very happy.

On first inspection, one could argue that the market (as measured by the performance of a portfolio of all equities listed on the New York Stock Exchange) has not done all that badly by its acolytes. For a family currently in the $26,000 tax bracket, the average return on the portfolio—dividends reinvested and adjusted for capital gains or losses—works out to a compounded annual rate of 8.3 percent for the half century ended Dec. 31, 1976.

Adjusted for inflation, however, the rate drops to 5.9 percent—no great reward for the risks of playing in a casino where almost half of the last 50 years have produced losses ranging anywhere from 2.2 percent to 47.8 percent. For a good chunk of that half-century, the cost of living was quite stable and the sharp scale-up of the income tax barely a threat over the political horizon.

Take the Fisher-Lorie results for the 15 years ended Dec. 31, 1976. The gross average annual return for that period was 7 percent. Adjusted for the harsh realities of commissions, inflation and taxes, however, the yield slips to only 1.2 percent for our family in the $26,000 tax bracket. For a family in a "high" income tax bracket, the return annualizes at exactly zero percent—zilch.

Bear markets are sometimes a matter of definition. But in the last 15 years, the Street has gone through at least three of them—1966, 1968-70 and 1973-74. For other long swings in that period, the market was moving sideways.

Since 1961 the level of attrition in the casino has been so high that the rate of return, adjusted for inflation, has been negative. As the University of Chicago professors note, this "disappointing result may help explain the net liquidation of mutual fund shares, the decline in the number of individuals investing in stocks, the low rate of net investment in plant, and equipment, and the low rate of economic growth in the United States."

Taking the casino as a whole, the odds are long, the payoff slim. Clearly there are long stretches when it is better to be in bonds or some other form of fixed-income securities than stocks. The Fisher-Lorie study demonstrates that timing switches from stocks to bonds (or vice versa) in an effort to maximize profits is a beach bleached white with the bones of failure. "Nobody," says Professor Fisher, "knows how to do it."

The Fisher-Lorie study tends to reinforce the so-called random walk or efficient market theory, which holds that a portfolio picked blindly by the hatpin or dartboard method is likely to do as well as a group of stocks researched by professionals. The market is so thoroughly scoured by brokerage firm analysts, the random walkers insist, that the price of a stock at any given moment reflects everything which is known about it. The consensus may change, but on the basis of current information no stock tends to be any better buy—or sale—than any other.

Most professionals, if only for the obvious reason that they have a vested interest in a market that is "knowable," insist that the random walkers are barking up the wrong average. On the whole, though, few of the professionals who run billions of dollars worth of pension fund and mutual fund assets have consistently managed to outperform the market. Badly burned by a "one decision" growth stock theory that pushed the I.B.M.s and Avons of this world to gaudy heights and then backfired, many institutional investors have turned to a new theory—indexing.

The theory is, in effect, a genuflection in the direction of the random walkers. Since no one can hope to do any better than the market, why not gear a portfolio to a replica of the market, do very little trading so as to cut down on commission costs, reduce research costs to a bare minimum, as well. Then, the argument goes, one will do at least as well as the market, and no worse.

Many Wall Streeters, including some whose track records are quite good, dismiss indexing as the worst kind of cop-out. Yet there is something to be said for it. Some theorists argue that playing the market is something like playing tennis—one should play not to win, but not to lose. Avoiding big losses is as important as picking winners. Thus a conservative individual investor could emulate the indexers by buying five to eight of the blue chips that weigh heavily in the averages, each in a different industry—say A.T. & T., Exxon, General Electric, General Motors, Johns Manville, Proctor & Gamble, Sears, and Union Carbide.

Using the index stocks as a base, a conservative investor might decide to move carefully into other more aggressive situations.

All of that, of course, begs the threshold question: should a person of moderate means who wants to enhance his net worth be in the stock market at all? My answer is yes, if you have the temperament. My answer is yes, because the market—with good judgment and some luck—is yet another way of trying to beat the twin scourges of the income tax and inflation. I think the random walkers and absolutely unassailable tests like the Fisher-Lorie study have taught us all humility. They have demonstrated that you have to be very careful of risks.

Except for all-out indexers, however, you don't buy the market. You buy individual stocks, and over the last decade many companies have consistently managed to outstrip inflation on two major counts: total return (price appreciation plus reinvested dividends) and earnings growth.

A recent compilation of more than 50 such companies by Merrill Lynch, for example, ranges from Aceto Chemical and Automatic Data Processing through J.P. Morgan and Ogilvy & Mather to Snap-On Tools and U.S. Tobacco.

Most such companies are marked by two characteristics—a comparatively high return on capital and a very high plowback of earnings into the business. Take McDonald's of the Golden Arch, probably the best-run company in the fast-food business. Over the last decade, it has consistently earned between 16 percent and 21 percent on stockholders investment. The company's dividend payout, though growing, has been minuscule. Virtually everything McDonald's earns gets recycled right back into new outlets. As a consequence net income since 1968 has shot from around $8.8 million to better than $160 million.

You can see the same pattern in Johnson & Johnson, the big drug producer. Since 1968, it has never earned less than 14.7 percent on net worth. Most of its cash has also gone back into the business, with the result that earnings since 1968 have wooshed from $49.7 million to close to $300 million.

Much of that build-up in earning power is tax-free and has translated into stock market prices that meant tax-preferred capital gains—gains which far outstripped inflation—for people who bought at the right time.

How do you go about finding such stocks? Well, past performance is not necessarily any guide to the future, but in my opinion you stand some chance of coming out ahead if you buy well-managed companies at comparatively low prices. That's a fundamentalist point of view, totally anathema to chartists who feel that the answer lies not so much in the basic position of a company as in the mysterious workings of the market itself.

Market action can't be ignored, but in my opinion elaborate price and volume charts can tell you only where the market has been, not where it is going. The important thing to remember is that the primary direction of the market pulls almost everything with it. In the 1972–74 bear market, for example, three out of every five stocks on both the New York Exchange and the American Exchange fell mor than 50 percent. Three out of every seven fell 70 percent or more. Carnage of that sort is one more argument for diversification. It is an argument for caution, but also opportunity's knock. The best time to buy stocks is not when every cocktail party is supercharged with bullish conversation about "The Market." Think like the Rothschilds. "The best time to buy . . . is when blood is running in the streets."

The strategy is to find companies with good growth records and to find them at the right price. The hope is that the market will ultimately catch up with the compounding effect of expanding earnings.

One prime resource that does all of the analytical work for you is the Value Line Investment Survey, located at 5 E. 44th Street, New York, N.Y. 10017. Available for study in many libraries and brokerage firm offices, the survey concentrates on more than 1,600 individual stocks. They are traded mainly, but not exclusively, on the New York Exchange.

The survey isolates in easily grasped form more than a score of vital operating statistics, including dividend payout, return on sales and total capital, the earnings plowback ratio and the price earnings ratio. The Value Line also measures the 1,600 issues it covers in terms of price volatility, safety, and timeliness.

There's lots more, but I think you should be your

own security analyst—at least to the point where you are able to sound a broker's recommendation or a hot tip from your internist for hollowness. Value Line helps to make it easy, though there are values to be had from Standard & Poor's Listed Stock Reports, as well. Generally speaking, a company that makes more on sales, more on capital, and plows most of its earnings back into the business is going to grow a lot faster than a company with less dynamic vital statistics.

The big consideration is price. You expect to pay more for a company with a good track record than for a clinker. The best statistical measure of what a company sells for lies in its price-earnings ratio. What are investors willing to pay for each dollar per share the company earns?

A company that earned $2 a share last year and sells for $20 a share is said to be trading at a P-E ratio or "multiple" of 10. A company that netted $3 a share and sells for $15 a share is trading at a multiple of five times earnings.

Putting the P-E ratio in perspective is a good way of avoiding mistakes. How does the current multiple compare with last year? With five years ago? How does it compare with the market as a whole? With other companies in the industry? The lower the multiple, the better off you are. I.B.M. was obviously a better buy recently when it was selling for 287 and 11.5 times earnings than when it was going for 365 a share and a multiple of 34 times earnings in 1973.

Fancy P-E ratios of 60 or thereabouts were all part of the excesses of the "one decision" growth stock craze of the 'sixties and early 'seventies. The one decision was to buy. Obviously, one would never sell such jewels as the "nifty fifty," some of which have since been bombed out to the point where they've almost become respectable buys again.

The excesses of the growth stock craze are one illustration of how the growing institutionalization of the market can hurt. In the main, the excesses can be laid at the doorstep of money managers (pension funds, mutual funds and the like), who with the gradual fading out of the individual investor now generate about two-thirds of all volume on the Big Board. The institutions still tend to trample one another getting in and out of stocks, and thereby add to their volatility. Modest institutional interest (say 5 percent to 10 percent of outstanding) is supportable and, in fact, may even help to reinforce your own convictions about the attractiveness of a stock. In general, though, be wary of issues in which the institutions loom big.

At one point not long ago, for example, Value Line warned that "institutional investors, owners of 34 percent of McDonald's shares, have been net sellers of the stock for the last 12 months. Nothing would be worse than if institutions bailed out en masse."

All of which brings us to a question of timing. P-E ratios are just part of the story. If a stock has had a long gain, don't buy it—even if you think there might be more mileage in it. If the market as a whole has had a long run-up, the inflation rate is high and interest rates are rising fast, forget the whole thing. If you can get 8 percent to 9 percent in Governments with no risk, why take unnecessary chances? You might miss the rest of a major market move, but remember that you're playing the game to avoid losing.

On the whole, one cheer for the stock market, but no one ever lost money through an excess of caution. If you've got long profits in a stock, take some of them—sell maybe as much as half. It's always nice to be playing with the casino's money.

If you'd like to get your feet wet in a modest way and in a social atmosphere that sometimes encourages a fruitful collision of investment ideas, why not think about joining—or starting—an investment club? Way back in 1972 when I.B.M. was trading at a juicy all-time high of $340 a share, there were more than 14,000 clubs with a total enrollment of 230,000 people on file with the National Association of Investment Clubs. The number has since shrunk to 5,000 clubs or so with a membership of about 70,000, but now appears to be on the upgrade again. There might be some virtue to joining the crowd.

TOP DOLLAR TIPS

(1) *If your cash reserves are thin or if your income is vulnerable to swings in the economy, think twice about putting any money at all in common stocks.*

(2) *For the conservative investor—a diversified blend of five to eight blue chips, souped up with an admixture of more aggressive situations.*

(3) *Things to look for—companies with fat profit*

margins, a high earnings plowback, and a low price-earnings ratio.

(4)   *If the market has had a long run-up, the inflation rate is high and interest rates are rising, it's time to take the money and run.*

Chapter 16

BUYING MUTUAL FUNDS

"Not everybody has a hot hand and nobody has a hot hand all the time," says Richard T. Cunniff, president of the Sequoia Fund. The description fits most money managers, including the Sequoia Fund itself, which has ranked among the very best mutual funds in some years, and taken a pounding in others.

Dick Cunniff will find no quarrel among the random walk theorists. True to their mordant view of life, they insist with some validity that the majority of money managers who do well one year are just as likely to do badly the next.

It's easy to see why. As Yale Hirsch, a song writer turned investment adviser notes in his authoritative

Mutual Funds Almanac, aggressive investment companies do well in bull markets, conservative ones better in bear markets. Few managers are able to track both with equally good results. Further, even in bull markets there are bound to be differences when the odds on turning a profit are a bit shorter for everyone. Mutual funds holding quality stocks are likely to do better in early phases of the market than in later ones when speculative issues become all the rage.

Yet it is clear that some mutual fund managers are better than others. *The Hirsch Mutual Funds Almanac* ($15, published annually by the Hirsch Organization, 6 Deer Trail, Old Tappan, N.J. 07675) monitors the performance of about 475 open-end investment companies—so-called because they continuously sell and stand ready to buy shares in themselves. The 1978 edition indicates that eight common funds have managed to hang on to rankings in the top 10 percent of all funds for at least four or five years. They are:

International Investors (5)
122 E. 42nd St.
New York, N.Y. 10017

Magellan Fund (5)
82 Devonshire Street
Boston, Mass. 02109

Templeton Growth
   Fund (5)
155 University Ave.
Toronto, M5H3B7, Canada

American Insurance &
   Industrial (4)
4333 Edgewood Road, N.E.
Cedar Rapids, Iowa 52406

Founders Special (4)
1300 First/Denver Plaza
Denver, Colo. 80217

Investors Selective (4)
1000 Roanoke Building
Minneapolis, Minn. 55402

Mutual Shares Corp. (4)   Pennsylvania Mutual
170 Broadway   Fund (4)
New York, N.Y. 10038   127 John St.
                                New York, N.Y. 10038

Consistency over four or five years is good shooting, but it is not a guarantee that the same funds will be dead on the bull's eye over the next four or five years. Other funds—sometimes simply because they've hit a handful of issues that really took off—have also done well by their shareholders over measured five-year periods. With mutual funds, though, as with any other kind of security, timing is crucial. For the most part, investors who bought into mutual funds at the bull market peak of 1972 are nursing the same capital losses they would have sustained if they'd put their money directly into stocks.

The size of some of those losses was appalling. Even such big, conservatively managed operations as the Dreyfus Fund dropped close to 20 percent in asset value during the great bear market of 1973–74. Industry wide, redemptions ran very high as stockholders cashed in their shares in what seemed to be one of the biggest mass revulsions against equities ever. The sharp cyclical swings in the market are among the reasons why only the very best (and most consistent) performing funds have been able to keep ahead of inflation.

For investors who want a chunk of the equity action and don't feel they can hack it on their own, mutual funds are an answer of sorts—but it's Catch 22 all over again. Mutual funds have to be selected just as carefully as you'd go about researching the direct purchase of a stock. Almost all mutual funds are structured the same way. Investors' dollars get channeled into a diversified pool of securities managed by an investment adviser who gets a fee of anywhere from ½ of 1 percent on down, depending on asset size. The hope is that the manager will be able to pick stocks that will increase in price, thereby enhancing the net asset value of investors' shares.

The hope is also that the adviser will, depending on the fund's objective, generate a stream of capital gains and/or dividend income that can be passed through to stockholders. Stock funds generally distribute at least 90 percent of their income because there are tax advantages to doing so. The dividends are taxed only once—to the shareholder—and not to the fund as well.

For most stock funds (bond funds are discussed in the chapter on bonds) the name of the game is capital gains. One of the industry's biggest sales tools is a kind of glory curve indicating how rapidly net asset values have increased over a standard 10- or 5-year period. As with all such comparisons, much depends on where you begin. A $10,000 investment in the Templeton Growth Fund in 1968, for example, would have been worth (with dividends and capital gains added) $60,696 ten years later. The same amount of money put into Mutual Shares Corp. would have been worth a little over $24,000. There are losers, too, of course—plenty of them. The same $10,000 put into the Scudder Special Fund in 1968, for example, would have been worth exactly $9,553 a decade later.

Put into the United Science Fund, the same $10,000 would have melted to $7,994.

For all of their variation in performance, one advantage the funds have to offer is diversification. A big fund might have a hundred or more issues in its portfolio and even a small one like the Lord Abbett Developing Growth Fund, Inc., has tucked shareholders' money into more than 40 different stocks. Few individual investors could duplicate that kind of diversification on their own. The effect is to spread the risk, an important consideration in a bear market, and to reduce volatility. Small funds—say under $50 million in assets—tend to be more volatile than big ones, but tend to have better performance records. With a small fund, it takes only a few good calls to make management look good. If you're managing the $1.4 billion Dreyfus Fund, on the other hand, it takes a lot of movement before the results begin to show.

Along with diversification, the funds offer the small investor an easy way to get started. A few major funds require initial minimum deposits of $1,000. Some insist on $500 or $250, but many require no minimum at all—either initially or on subsequent investments.

An investor of modest means can get started in the American Insurance and Industrial Fund, for example, with as little as $10 down and a minimum of $10 for each subsequent order. Thus, the funds do offer a convenient way to invest regularly on a comparatively convenient basis. Some investment companies charge sales commissions of 8 percent or more—"load" funds in the argot of the Street—and some do not. The commission can hurt because it eats into the amount of capital you have at work. For every $100 you put up, you get only $92 worth of shares. With the "no load" funds, all of the cash is invested. Over the long haul, that can make quite a difference, and increasingly the industry is shifting from a load to a no-load basis.

The following examples, provided by Yale Hirsch, show why. The comparison is load versus no-load, with both funds initially at net asset values of $10 a share. The first example assumes a 10 percent gain in the Dow Jones industrials; the second a 10 percent decline. Both examples assume an 8 percent sales charge on the load fund.

EXAMPLE 1 (Dow advances 10 percent, from 1,000 to 1,100)

	Load Fund	No Load Fund
Net Asset Value/Share with Dow 1,000	$10.00	$10.00
Offering Price to Investor	10.80	10.00
Net Asset Value/Share with Dow 1,100	11.00	11.00
Redemption Price	11.00	11.00
Profit	.20	1.00
Percentage Profit	1.9%	10.0%

EXAMPLE 2 (Dow declines 10 percent, from 1,000 to 900)

	Load Fund	No Load Fund
Net Asset Value/Share with Dow 1,000	10.00	10.00
Offering price to investor	10.80	10.00
Net Asset Value/Share with Dow 900	9.00	9.00
Redemption Price	9.00	9.00
Loss	1.80	1.00
Percentage Loss	16.7%	10.0%

Many commentators argue the difference is so substantial that you should invest only in no-loads. The sales commission tends to hold investors in a load fund, whereas if you are in a no-load there are no acquisition costs to keep you from switching freely from fund to fund as performance changes.

There is some merit to that argument. With a load fund, you start off behind the market and Yale Hirsch has found that no-loads have "outperformed loads over a period of years." About a score of the no-loads do charge a 1 percent or 2 percent redemption if you cash in your shares, mainly because they want to discourage short term traders from taking advantage of swings in net asset value. Should you be discouraged by a fund with a redemption fee? Probably not. The fee is a comparatively modest one, as commissions go. Should you be turned off completely by a full front-end load? Probably, but there are some load funds—both the Pioneer Fund and Pioneer 11, for example (28 State St., Boston, Mass. 02109)—whose performance has consistently compensated for the drag of the initial load.

Among the best performing no-loads at this writing are:

Mutual Shares Corp.
170 Broadway
New York, N.Y. 10038

Hamilton Income Fund
3600 S. Yosemite St.
Denver, Colo. 80237

Sequoia Fund
540 Madison Ave.
New York, N.Y. 10022

Evergreen Fund
600 Mamaroneck Ave.
Harrison, N.Y. 10528

Financial Industrial Income
   Fund
P.O. Box 2040
Denver, Colo. 80201

How do you measure performance? By calculating changes in net asset value over a period of time, either adding in dividends and capital gains, or taking them (as most people do in real life) in additional shares. The financial pages of most major newspapers carry the net asset values of most major mutual funds. There are several other publications besides the *Mutual Funds Almanac* which will spare you the calculations and give you performances at a glance. *Forbes* magazine (60 Fifth Avenue, New York, N.Y. 10011) rates the funds annually in its August 15 issue. The *Forbes* presentation is particularly useful because it ranks the funds in both up and down markets, an important test of consistency. *Barron's National Business and Financial Weekly*, also available at the newsstands, rates the funds quarterly. The bible of the industry is the *Weisenberger Services Annual Investment Company Survey*, available in many libraries and brokerage firm offices. Lipper Analytical Services, 74 Trinity Place, New York, N.Y. 10048, also available at many brokerage firms, keeps regular tabs on the funds' performance, too.

Some background reading is a must. Also on the must list is a thorough study of the fund's prospectus, annual and quarterly reports. The prospectus will tell you what the fund's operating expenses are, show you what the fund is invested in, and what it has been buying and selling. And most of all, the prospectus will tell you what the fund's investment objectives are. If your objective is long term growth, you certainly don't want to put your money in a fund whose goal is generating lots of current income. How much risk do you want to take and what kind of potential rewards are you looking for? The higher the potential rewards, the longer the risks.

Distinctions between fund objectives tend to get fuzzed out in the growth-performance area, but what follows—thanks to the *Mutual Funds Almanac*—is a delineation of the traditional lines along which the principal types of stock funds fall:

● Long Term Growth Funds, as the name suggests, concentrate on companies that appear to have the best long term growth prospects. They carry risks that vary with size and portfolio turnover—the smaller the fund, the bigger the risk; the higher the rate of turnover, the higher the degree of risk.

● Performance Funds, a more aggressive variant of the growth funds, set their sights on maximum capital gains. They tend to be comparatively small (under $100 million), and often concentrate on comparatively unseasoned "emerging" growth companies trading at low multiples. The performance funds tend to be a rather volatile lot.

● Growth-Income Funds seek a blend of long term growth and current income and are more conservative in their approach than the straight-out all growth funds.

● Income Funds are for investors looking for a high current return on their money. They split into two sub-groups—flexibly diversified funds which spread their assets over a mix of common stocks, preferred stocks and bonds, and outright bond funds.

There is a clutch of other somewhat more specialized open-ends—industry funds that concentrate on insurance stocks, some form of chemical stocks (The Chemical Fund), or some form of energy companies (The Energy Fund). There are even social conscience funds for people who don't want their money invested in no-no's such as cigarette companies, distillers or armament producers. There are even funds that invest exclusively in the shares of other mutual funds, which may be the ultimate in diversification.

Most major open-end management companies work for a family of funds. Each fund in the family usually has different objectives. If your objective changes or if you find another fund in the family is performing better because of changes in the market, it is possible to switch from one to another without paying an additional load. A $5 service charge for such a move, however, is not uncommon.

TOP DOLLAR TIPS

(1) Search for mutual funds that have demonstrated consistently good results over a period of years.

(2) Small funds tend to be riskier, but often have better track records than the biggies.

(3) On the whole, no-load funds are a better investment buy than load funds.

(4) Before you buy, make sure a fund's investment objectives are the same as your own.

Chapter 17

SELECTING INVESTMENT ADVICE

The stock market gets more analytical poking and prodding than the daily intake at the Mayo Clinic. Every day brings tons more of the stuff, ranging from once-over-lightly newspaper *rapportage* to inch-thick soundings of the utilities industry and the like from such research-oriented operations as Goldman, Sachs.

The quality of the advice ranges the spectrum. Much of it is junk, some of it is useful in the sense that it might keep you from making mistakes, but virtually none of it is the dream stuff from which capital gains are made.

It's true that some advisory service with a large

following might make a temporary dent in the market from time to time. But few advisers—or managers—can manage to outdistance the curse of the random walk theory for very long. Much of the research that comes out of brokerage firms, in fact, is essentially sales promotion material—a spreading of the wares, as it were, designed to stimulate commissions business.

As Peter Mazonas, head of the Bank of America's executive financial counseling service, puts it: "In the typical pattern a stock is . . . accumulated at bargain prices by market professionals and semi-professional traders (and) . . . held until it can be distributed to the public at higher prices." The Bank of America executive continues, "After distribution, the price of the stock is marked down with the help of professional selling."

Given the dubious quality of most money managers' performance over the last decade, that statement may be giving the professionals a bit too much credit. Most advisory services have not done any better, but they are more than willing (at a price) to help you try to improve your luck. The Big Three—Standard & Poor's Outlook, Value Line, and the United Business and Investments Report—are, in my opinion, the most helpful for the investor who wants to be his own security analyst. Of the three, I would give the edge to Value Line, but all three concentrate on fundamentals.

There is a slew of other more specialized services. They range from such flow of funds technicians as T.J. Holt, whose twice monthly Holt Investment Advisory

(277 Park Avenue, New York, N.Y. 10017) has called several major turns in the market, to such Dow Theory interpreters as Richard Russell's Dow Theory Letters, Inc. (P.O. Box 1759, La Jolla, Calif. 92038), and John Westergaard's Equity Research Associates (30 Rockefeller Plaza, New York, N.Y. 10020), which focuses on small (sales of less than $100 million) "emerging" growth companies. Many such services sell for $150 a year and up; most offer short trial periods for a whole lot less.

Are they worth the price? For the average individual investor, probably no more than most professional managers. Some services at least stimulate thought. You have to get your ideas from somewhere, but in the end the decision to buy or sell has to come from you. You still have to make choices, and there is no guarantee that one is going to be any better than another.

There is a large element of the subjective in the whole business. What kind of an adviser should you choose? "Tell me what you want," says James W. Michaels, the astute editor of *Forbes* magazine, in his customary Socratic way. "Do you want a bull, or a bear?"

There seem to be fewer charlatans in the business now than a number of years ago when one astrologer-adviser who purported to make his market picks on the basis of the stars was found actually to have been basing his research on Standard & Poor's Outlook. He was put under strict injunction by the New York State Attorney General not to purvey market advice, as long as he advertised it that way, unless the stuff truly came from the stars.

The advisory field sometimes still does have a zany feel about it. Almost anyone can set up shop as an adviser. There are no particular qualifications needed. The one requirement is that an adviser spell out his pedigree with the Securities & Exchange Commission on form ADV.

All such files are public information. The credentials can be checked at the S.E.C. office in the region where the adviser does business (26 Federal Plaza in New York City for the New York-New Jersey region, for example), or by writing directly to the agency's public reference section at 500 North Capitol Street, S.E., Washington, D.C. 20549. A form ordered from Washington costs 15 cents a page, with a maximum charge of $2 at this writing, and takes about three weeks to be processed. Advisers must detail such items as education and business background.

Credentials and personal background aside, it helps to know something about an adviser's batting average. What sort of buys and sells has he recommended? How well has he done over the last year—in written detail—against such accepted measures as the S. & P. 500 stock average?

In general, the law requires that advisers act in a fashion that is "not misleading." Thus, when an adviser trumpets his successes, he also has to pinpoint his failures. All of his recommendations for 12 months back are supposed to be an open book, and fair game for any client who wants to get a line on his competence.

Basically, most advisers and money managers are looking for the same thing, stocks with a story—

undervalued earnings, a court judgment that might fill company coffers with a big cash settlement, enhanced patent protection, a take-over bid at well over the going market.

Insiders and those close to them have that information first, but secrets are hard to keep. Most of the thousands of analysts tend to concentrate on the same list of 250 stocks or so. As Yale Hirsch notes, the efforts of the analysts and informed laymen "tend to neutralize each other" because of the comparatively limited terrain over which they operate. About 1,600 companies are listed on the Big Board. Another 1,200 are listed on the American Exchange and there are about 10,000 actively traded issues in the sprawling over-the-counter market.

Despite that rich range of choice, Hirsch continues, "most institutional money goes into relatively few listed stocks." "As a practical matter," he adds, "it may be very well impossible for any one professional to consistently outperform his fellows."

That seems to me a good argument for concentrating on the less "efficient" over-the-counter market— less efficient in the sense that it is not dominated by institutional investors or their analysts, and thus more likely to offer opportunity to the discerning eye.

The over-the-counter market is so big that nobody can know everything about it. The name springs from the nature of the market. Stocks are bought and sold through dealers on a bid and ask basis (check the financial pages of your favorite newspaper) rather than through the continuous auction process traditional on the Big Board and Amex. OTC companies run the gamut from the most fledgling that have just gone public for the first time to such well-entrenched giants as Anheuser-Busch. Traditionally it has been the place to catch growth companies on the way up, while they are still comparatively cheaply priced and have yet to be taken up by the institutions.

Some counter stocks, it is true, are already the subject of heavy institutional interest. More than 40 percent of the outstanding stock of Ogilvy & Mather International, for example, one of the most profitable and fastest growing advertising agencies in the trade, is held by institutional investors. The institutions also own about 40 percent of the opinion-sounding A.C. Nielsen Co., and better than 30 percent of that sainted purveyor of groceries, S.S. Pierce & Co. The significance of the institutions' presence is that they've been able to sniff out solid growth records at lower prices than comparable stocks on the Big Board.

That hasn't always been the case. The OTC market has run amok with rank speculation, too. During the 'sixties, rabid crapshooters bid up almost everything in sight—especially anything that seemed to have a high technology handle on it. Then, it was almost as though someone, somewhere, had pulled a gigantic plug. Almost everything got washed down the drain, and it was a long time before the market really began to come back some.

There is no guarantee that the bust side of the cycle won't erupt all over again at some point in the future, just as it did in late 1978. In fact, it almost certainly will. Tulipmania has been known to strike more than once in the same place. On the whole, the counter market is a riskier arena than the Big Board. Small companies on the make, many of them underfinanced, are terribly vulnerable to shifts in demand, turns in the economy, and sudden increases in competitive pressure.

Their shares tend to be quite volatile, too. Because big blocks of the stock are often held by insiders, the float (the number of shares available for public trading) tends to be thin. Thus, it often takes very little buying or selling to make counter stocks move. That's one of the reasons why the institutional presence is not so heavy. The best of the big investors like stocks they can move in and out of in size without disturbing the market. The risks are high, but so are the potential rewards

What to look for? Consider some of the bargains that have been snapped up by such performance oriented open-end investment companies as the Acorn Fund and the Sequoia Fund.

Both funds pay more attention to the counter market than most and have put together an envious string of asset gains by doing so. One big consideration, of course, are P-E ratios in the four to six times range. Other criteria: a good growth record, some dividend payout, little or no debt, and strong cash positions.

Take the Acorn Fund and one of its big gainers, Houston Oil & Minerals Corp. Acorn's adjusted price on the stock, which it began buying in 1973, is $2 to $3 a share. Houston Oil subsequently sold for better than $30 a share. What was the attraction? "It looked undervalued," says Ralph Wanger, president of the

Acorn Fund. "It was trading at a very modest multiple, had made an important new discovery in the Bolivar field off Galveston Bay, and it was fairly clear that good exploration teams were going to transform the earnings."

Or take the Sequoia Fund and Booth Newspapers. Sequoia bought up a chunk of the midwest newspaper chain at an average cost of $10 a share. One of journalism's most omnivorous entrepreneurs, Sam Newhouse, subsequently bought up the Booth stock for $47 a share. What did Sequoia see in the company?

"Booth had a considerable amount of excess cash to begin with," says Richard Cunniff, president of Sequoia. "It was selling well below book value, it was cheap in terms of earning power, and we concluded it was worth a helluva lot more than the market was saying."

There are other mutual funds that concentrate on the counter market, notably the Over-the-Counter Securities Fund, Inc. (Oreland, Pa. 19075), which has also run up a good performance record in the last decade by focusing on fundamental values.

The same fundamental approach can be followed with small companies in your neighborhood, companies that you already know something about, or can learn something about simply by talking to people who work there. Good basic sources of information on counter stocks include Standard & Poor's, Moody's, and the *OTC Review,* a monthly magazine published by Ralph P. Coleman, Jr., who is also head of the OTC Securities Fund.

As a do-it-yourself investor, you really aren't tied to

the umbilical of your broker's research. If that's the case, why pay for what you're not going to use? Yet you do just that every time you pay a commission. Research is just one of the costs of doing business that gets passed on to the client. Standard commissions can hurt. If you buy 100 shares of a stock selling for $25, for example, the cost will be $48.95. That means you need almost a half-point just to break even, and as much again if you're going to sell.

Heavy pressure from big institutional investors and the Securities & Exchange Commission destroyed the old fixed commission schedule on May 1, 1975. In the Wall Street rhetoric, it was a day of infamy, appropriately called "Mayday" after the international distress signal. With rates set by naked competition for the first time ever, institutional investors benefited handsomely. Transaction costs in some cases were pushed to as low as a nickel a share. There is no question that the new dispensation added impetus to the wave of mergers which has swept the Street. Big individual investors—those generating $5,000 or more a year in commissions—began thumping on the table for lower rates, too, and got them. Who took up the slack? Small individual investors, who in most cases these days are paying higher commissions than back in the old fixed rate days.

That discrimination helped to create a vacuum that a new breed of discount brokers, some of them Big Board members, were only too happy to fill.

The new breed are plain pipe rack operators—no research, no hand-holding registered reps, just plain old order taking and execution. There are some fringes. Most discount brokers insure customer accounts, in amounts ranging to as much as $500,000. Most discount brokers—there are more than 40 in the field—also offer margin accounts.

Some discounters want money up front before they begin cutting anywhere from 30 percent to as much as 80 percent off the old standard rates. The discounters are not for everybody. If you are a casual trader, say no more than five small transactions a year, there is probably no particular advantage in going to the discounters. Most demand minimums of $25 and up per trade. The typical discount customer, according to Forbes magazine, probably logs 15 or more trades a year, and tends to deal in fairly sizable lots of 500 to 1,000 shares.

One easy way to reduce your transaction costs to an absolute minimum is to join one of the dividend reinvestment plans offered by more than 800 of the nation's biggest companies, ranging from A.T.&T. and Bristol-Myers Co. to Long Island Lighting and F.W. Woolworth.

At least 40 companies, mainly capital hungry utilities like A.T.&T., permit shareholders (a) to reinvest their dividends in more stock and make optional additional payments of up to $12,000 a year at no charge; and (b) credit the stock bought through dividend reinvestment (but not optional payments) at a discount of 5 percent below the market. That's a good deal all around. By selling new shares, even at a 5 percent discount, the companies assure themselves of a relatively cheap and continuous source of new capital. Almost a quarter of A.T.&T.'s huge shareholder family, for example, recycle their dividends back into the company to the tune of better than a half billion dollars a year. That figure also includes optional payments.

The plans vary. Some companies, instead of selling new shares à la A.T.&T., have an agent buy the shares in the open market at the going price. The agent is usually a bank. Citibank and the Morgan Guaranty Trust Company are among the biggest in the field. The charges vary, too, from as little as 2 percent and a maximum fee of $2, up to 5 percent and a maximum fee of $2.50 for each investment. The banks hold the shares in safekeeping, thereby saving a lot of paper shuffling, but will issue them to you at any time on request.

The acquisition costs in the reinvestment plans are cheaper by far than on comparable purchases through a broker, and have the added virtue of letting your dividends compound for you. Should you sign up for a dividend reinvestment plan? By all means, as long as you don't need the extra cash to live on and the stock seems to be a good buy.

Among the major discount brokers located in New York City are: Marquette de Bary Co.; Kingsley, Boye & Southwood; Quick & Reilly; Shearman, Ralston; Muriel Siebert & Co.; and Source Securities.

Discount brokers located outside New York City include Burke, Christensen & Lewis Securities, Inc., Chicago; Daley, Collidge & Co., Cleveland, Ohio; Kahn & Co., Inc., Memphis, Tenn.; Charles Schwab & Co., San Francisco, Calif.; Springer Investment & Securities Co., Inc., Indianapolis, Ind.; and StockCross,

Boston, Mass. Quick & Reilly has a number of branches outside New York, including Baltimore, Md., Miami and Palm Beach, Fla., and Washington, D.C.

TOP DOLLAR TIPS

(1) If you're in doubt about an investment adviser's basic credentials, check his pedigree with the Securities & Exchange Commission.

(2) Every adviser has to spell out his batting average. He can talk about his home runs, but he has to tell you about the number of times he has struck out, too.

(3) The best place to look for emerging growth companies on the make, at comparatively low prices, is in the over-the-counter market.

(4) Some of the best buys may be among the companies with dividend reinvestment programs that enable you to acquire stock at a 5 percent discount.

Chapter 18

STOCKS
AT A
DISCOUNT

In some respects closed-end investment companies are the antimacassars of Wall Street, relicts of the days when investors were content to put their money in the hands of Lehman Brothers or other old line managers and watch it grow. They still have a fair amount of bulk, being about 50 in number with total assets of more than $6 billion. But the closed-ends are something of a financial backwater despite the fact they offer a way of buying stocks and bonds at discounts that range to 20 percent or more.

In many cases the closed-ends—Lehman Corp., the Madison Fund and Tri-Continental Corp., for example—are a way to buy at well below the market a broad, diversified list of common stocks that can be had in comparable open-end investment companies only with the payment of an 8 percent sales charge. The major differences between the two forms of investment companies are structural.

The closed-end companies have a fixed capitalization. They do not continuously sell shares in themselves—a characteristic which spares them the embarrassment of the heavy redemptions that have plagued the mutual funds, but at the same time limits their growth. Another difference is that the closed-ends are traded in an auction market—mainly the Big Board—while the open-ends, of course, are sold directly. When you buy closed-end shares, you pay regular Big Board commissions on them at rates that are a good deal lower than the 8 percent exacted on purchases of load funds.

The mechanism of the market place gives rise to the discount. Most closed-ends have traditionally traded at discount, though a few—Petroleum Corp. of America, which invests only in the oil industry; and ASA, Ltd., which specializes in South African gold issues—often sell at a premium. The discount (or premium) lies in the spread between the market price of the underlying shares and the pro-rata asset value of the securities in the closed-end company's portfolio.

For the sake of this discussion, let's assume that Lehman Corp. is currently trading at $9.87 a share and that its net asset value is $13.50 a share. That's a discount of 27 percent. Or say that Tri-Continental Corp. is selling at $18 a share and has a net asset value of $22.50. That's a discount of 19.8 percent.

Lehman, with total assets of around $400 million, and Tri-Con, with assets of around $590 million, are the biggest in the business and more or less typify the diversified common stock funds. Their portfolios tend to read like a list of the Fortune 500. Their objective is conservative growth.

Besides ASA, Ltd., and its gold stocks and Petroleum Corp. and its oil stocks, however, there are a number of other specialized equity companies in the field. Japan Fund, as the name suggests, concentrates on Japanese securities. The Bancroft Convertible Fund focuses on bonds, preferred stocks, and other securities that can be switched into common stock. As you'll see in Chapter 20, there are also closed-ends that specialize in bonds.

You can usually count on two or three of the closed-end funds, though not always the same ones, to pop up on the *Forbes* honor roll of best performing investment companies. On the whole, though, most of the big closed-ends have done no better in protecting their shareholders against inflation than have the open-ends. What makes the closed-ends interesting, though, is the discount. The spread between the asset value of closed-ends and their market value is the key to what can be a useful trading strategy. It all turns on what Thomas J. Herzfeld, executive vice-president of Bishop, Rosen & Co., Inc., and one of the few analysts to specialize in the closed-ends, calls an "excessively large discount." The point of the exercise is to buy when the discount deepens, and sell when it narrows.

The discount, of course, varies from fund to fund.

By "excessively large" Mr. Herzfeld means a deviation of about 5 percent below the norm for aggressive investors and about 10 percent for more conservative ones. All of that costs commissions, of course.

And the commission costs add to the seriousness involved in making sure that the discount is deep enough to play with. In one case, for example, Mr. Herzfeld says he put his clients into the Madison Fund at 8⅝ a share, a discount of 31.9 percent, at a time when the Dow Jones industrial averages were at 818. Over the next five months, the averages rose to 1,002. Moving even faster than the market, the fund's portfolio value climbed to $16.52 a share, an increase of 30 percent. As the market and net asset value moved, the discount narrowed to about 20 percent and the price of Madison Fund went to $13 a share. That was a gain of 51 percent on a market move of 22.5 percent, and does not include the 30 cents a share the fund paid out in dividends during the period.

Everything was working on that one. Like everyone else in the Street, Mr. Herzfeld has his failures, too. But he argues that hitting the discounts right in a rising market can provide a lot of leverage. In a down market, the discount can provide a kind of cushion—but sometimes it goes right on deepening. That's the risk factor.

The Miami, Fla., based analyst sounds a note of caution. "If the normal discount is not judged correctly," he says, "it can work as much against the investor as for him." "Also," he adds, "not all funds' net asset values move exactly proportionately to the market. Therefore, it is essential for a trader to be familiar with the historical performance and current portfolios of any fund he considers trading."

Current discount figures on the closed-ends can be found weekly in *The Wall Street Journal*, in the financial pages of *The New York Times* and other major newspapers. So can yield figures. The same basic sources of information on mutual funds (*The Mutual Funds Almanac*, et al.) are also chock-a-block with stats on the closed-ends.

The discount is paramount, but there are other things to check out. To Mr. Herzfeld's way of thinking, they include the following:

● A comparative reading of the quality and liquidity of the fund's portfolio.

● A rating of the fund's management performance, the size of management fees, and the level of portfolio turnover.

● The level of debt, if any, in the capital structure and the volatility of the stock.

All of those elements impact in some way on the discount at which the fund trades. Mr. Herzfeld, in fact, gets his notion of what a "normal discount" is by constructing a moving average of the discounts on each closed-end he follows. He factors all of the variables into the equation by a top secret formula that is as closely guarded as Julia Child's recipe for five alarm chili.

It is hard to isolate exactly how much variables such as management performance have to do with the size of the discount at which a fund trades. Theories about the reasons for the cut rates abound. Some argue the discounts are a function of the potential tax liabilities stockholders absorb on unrealized portfolio gains.

Still others insist the discount reflects brokers' unwillingness to put any hard sell behind relatively unromantic securities on which commissions are smaller than mutual funds, say, or options.

Whatever the reasons, the discount has made a number of closed-end funds real or potential takeover candidates. The strategy, as developed by Keith Gollust, his partner Ben Jacobson and a number of other entrepreneurs, is to profit by wiping out the discount. Messrs. Gollust and Jacobson got interested in closed-ends several years ago when they were working in the corporate finance department of White, Weld & Co., an old line investment banking house since absorbed by Merrill Lynch. Their approach is to eliminate the discount at the stroke of a pen, as it were, by simply forcing a change in the structure of the fund from closed to open-end. The change means, of course, that the fund will begin redeeming its shares at net asset value.

At one point recently, for example, when the Gollust-Jacobson combine was making a successful run at National Aviation & Technology Corp., the fund was trading on the Big Board at $20.50 a share. The net asset value was $24.36 a share, for a discount of 15.9 percent. The discount had been even deeper before the Gollust-Jacobson group and other professionals began putting the pressure on. The effect of that pressure is an immediate profit on the difference between the price at which a closed-end is bought and its net asset value.

The pressure from capital gains oriented outsiders is building to the point where a number of managements have decided to jump before they get pushed. The United Corporation, for instance, expunged its discount by merging with Baldwin-United, a conglomerator's delight of musical instruments, insurance, savings and loan, and banking services.

Advance Investors, a closed-end common stock faced with a deepening discount because of the buffeting its growth stock portfolio took, also bit the bullet and converted into a no-load open-end fund. Redemptions were heavy as stockholders took the money and ran.

The prospect of open-ending is something of a kicker for closed-end investors. It's no secret in Wall Street that a number of such funds are on somebody or other's hit list. What companies are most vulnerable? Those with the deepest discounts, certainly. But other elements that can be exploited include poor investment performance, high operating expenses, and modest insider holdings.

"A bad track record is an important consideration," says Mr. Herzfeld. "When a company has not been doing well, investors these days are quick to look for alternatives."

TOP DOLLAR TIPS

(1)   Closed-end investment companies offer a way to buy stocks at a discount.

(2) Keep your eye on the level of the discounts. If they widen, closed-ends may be a good buy.

(3) Discount is important, but it helps to check out such items as management performance, management fees and portfolio turnover, too.

(4) Look for really deep discount take-over possibilities that can be sold out at a profit.

Chapter 19

PREFERRED STOCKS

"Preferred stocks are being sold, not bought, if you know what I mean," says Dan Campbell, head of the Loeb Rhoades Hornblower preferred stock department. Thanks in part to the generous underwriting commissions corporations have been willing to pay, Wall Street has been moving huge blocks of preferred stocks into the hands of individual investors.

The primary market for preferred stocks, so called because they have a higher claim to dividends than common stocks, used to be institutional. Disenchantment with equities and the switch to a more income-oriented strategy, however, have created a big upsurge of interest in preferreds. The interest among individual investors is so great, in fact, that Merrill Lynch and other big brokerage firms have been selling preferred stock unit trusts on almost an assembly line basis.

What's the big attraction? Preferred stocks, after all—like convertible bonds—are a kind of hybrid. The fixed dividends preferreds pay—$8 a year, or 8 percent on a $100 per share, for example—are established in terms of what is happening in the bond market at the time they are first issued. Preferred prices—and yields—move pretty much in synchrony with prices and yields in the bond market. If interest rates go up, preferred prices are likely to go down, and vice versa.

Yet preferreds are a kind of ugly duckling. They do have a claim to a fixed dividend, but not to company assets. They therefore lack the security of a bond. Preferreds generally carry no voice in the management of a company and, with certain exceptions, cannot share in the increased earning power of a company. They therefore lack the advantages of common stock. Mainly what they have to offer is a higher degree of safety and stability than common stocks. And preferreds do have one advantage for the income-seeking individual investor who might not want to put up $1,000 for a bond.

Preferred stocks sell in some relation to the par value at which they were originally issued—traditionally $100, but increasingly of late, as part of the appeal to individual investors, $50 or $25 or even $10. Many preferred stocks trade on the Big Board in round lot units of 10 shares, which makes them generally cheaper and easier to buy and sell than an odd lot (less than 10) of bonds.

Preferred stocks are rated in the same way as bonds—from AAA on down—but their yields are generally lower. Preferred returns should fit somewhere in the spectrum between bonds and common stocks, but there are times when common stock yields are higher. Thus, the first thing to check out with a preferred is where it stands in the pecking order of return.

Logically, preferred stocks should yield more than bonds. They are riskier than bonds. If a management misses a bond payment, it faces the possibility of being thrown into bankruptcy. Not so with preferred dividends. They can be omitted with impunity. Bonds have a fixed maturity. Short of a default, bond holders are sure of getting their capital back.

Preferred stocks have no fixed maturity and are subject totally to the quicksilver of the marketplace. There is absolutely no money back guarantee. Those are all heavy risks to take. My advice is not to buy a preferred that yields less than a bond, assuming both carry the same quality rating.

The risk-reward relationship between some bonds and preferreds is thrown out of kilter by a wrinkle in the tax laws. As with common stock, preferred dividends are fully taxable to the individual investor. On the theory that dividends ought not to be taxed twice, however, corporate investors are levied on only 15 percent of the dividend income they receive. Thus, if a company is in the 48 percent tax bracket, the tax collector gets only a bit more than seven cents out of every dividend dollar the corporation takes in. The tax break, along with their comparatively low market risk, makes preferreds a great favorite of corporate treasurers with spare cash to invest. Their eagerness to buy—and the higher net return they get because of the tax break—is one of the reasons why many preferreds yield less than bonds.

Corporate investors will rarely reach below an A rating. That's a sound tactic for individuals to follow, too. There are some other items on the checklist. Make sure that the preferred is cumulative—i.e., that any dividends omitted must be added to future dividends and paid before common stockholders get any money. As with bonds, take a look at the kind of protection you're getting against either a call (retirement by the company) or a refinancing if rates happen to turn against you. With most preferreds there is a grace period of five to ten years, and the call prices are at a premium.

The size of the premium, of course, is inevitably a reflection of the tug of war between the investment quality of a company, the state of the money market, and how much sweetener management feels it has to exchange to get the capital it wants.

Sometimes the sweetener comes in the form of the right to convert the preferred into common stock. The convertibility factor usually means that the investor will have to give up some yield as a trade-off against the prospect of turning a profit on a run-up in the underlying common.

As with convertible bonds, there are two ways to win—and two ways to lose. If the stock market goes up and/or interest rates go down, you win. If the stock market goes down and/or interest rates go up, you lose. With convertibles, parity is the base line. It is the balance point where the price of the convertible exactly equals the value of the shares into which it can be exchanged.

Take a preferred trading at $100. If it converts into four common shares, each of which is selling at $25, there is stasis: 4 x 25 = 100. When a convertible trades above parity, it is selling at a premium. If it trades below parity, the convertible is selling at a discount. Most convertibles tend to trade at a premium because they generally (but not always) offer a higher yield than the underlying common. Premiums usually narrow if the common stock rises, and get fatter if the common declines. The professionals are great premium watchers. One conservative rule of thumb is not to touch a convertible that trades at a premium of more than 10 percent.

The professionals—banks, casualty insurance companies and the like—are also choosy when it comes to quality. The higher grade preferreds tend to gravitate to the institutional investors, often by direct placement, while the medium-to-lower grade deals get packaged into public offerings. One merchandising ploy has been the switch from $100 to $25 (and sometimes lower) par issues. The change was designed to make it easier to sell 200 and 300 share round lots to individual investors.

Some fairly heavy merchandising has also gone into the sale of preferred stock unit trusts. Everything we've said about the workings of bond unit trusts applies to the preferred unit trusts. Essentially, they are tweedledum and tweedledee, except for one thing. Some unit trust sponsors, in their reach for yield, seem to stretch the preferred portfolio quality a bit thinner than the bond portfolios. The diversification a unit trust can offer is nice, but not at any price. As the man said, "Preferred stocks are bought, not sold," and we do know what he means.

TOP DOLLAR TIPS

(1)   The only reason for buying a preferred stock is yield. What kind of a return can you get in relation to common stocks and bonds?

(2)   Preferreds might be a good buy for a corporation because their dividends qualify for an 85 percent tax exclusion.

(3)   As with bonds, never reach below an A rating with preferreds unless you're in a really speculative frame of mind.

(4)   Be wary of low par ($25 and $10) preferreds. They may be short on quality and the subject of a heavy selling campaign. What's good for a registered rep's commission income is not necessarily good for you.

Chapter 20

BONDS

The bond market is a loose term that encompasses more than $900 billion—everything from the U.S. Treasury's "Centuries" (so called because they mature in the year 2000) to "Peggy" (the 30-year 12 percent securities of the Public Service Electric & Gas Co.).

For the most part, the market is institutional. Pension funds, insurance companies, and banks all have the cash and staying power to stick with bonds that may not mature for another 40 years. The last decade has seen an extraordinary rise in interest rates, though, in what is mainly the reflection of the Government's less than efficacious efforts to halt inflation. From 1925 to 1965, in fact, the best investment grade industrial bonds never got above 5 percent, and there were long periods when investors were getting as little as 2 percent or 3 percent on their money.

In 1968, Triple A bonds broke the 6 percent barrier for the first time, and since then have been swinging between 7 percent and better than 9 percent. Those yields were so much higher than could be got in a savings bank that individual investors began to discover the bond market in a big way. There was so much interest in the blend of income and safety that open-end bond funds began to proliferate like rabbits in a magician's hat. Some of the funds specialize in corporate bonds, others in tax-exempt municipals (see Chapter 22).

The primary objective of the 24 million Americans who own bonds of one kind or another is safety. Bonds are I.O.U.s backed either by specific assets or the full faith and credit of the issuer. Bondholders have a first claim on the earnings of a company. The idea is that you get all your money back when the bond matures. Safety, of course, is a highly relative term. The wreck of the Penn Central proved that. A company's ability to pay off on its bonds is no better than its basic earning power. The quality of that earning power is the first thing to check out.

How much debt does the company have outstanding? Does it make enough money to cover its interest costs by a handy margin? All of those considerations, and more, are taken into account by the number-crunchers at the two major bond rating agencies—Standard & Poor's and Moody's. Ratings aren't everything, but they provide a quick, handy guide to the quality of a bond.

Here's how the hierarchy stacks up:

Investment Quality	Moody's	S. & P.
Prime	Aaa	AAA
Excellent	Aa	AA
Upper Medium	A-1*	
	A	A
Lower Medium	Baa-1*	
	Baa	BBB
Marginally Speculative	Ba	BB
Very Speculative	B	
	Caa	B
Default	Ca	
	C	D

*Municipal Bonds Only

Moody's tends to be a little more conservative than Standard & Poor's, but the analytical techniques are pretty much the same everywhere. Bond ratings are not infallible, however, nor are they graven in stone. Plenty of other analysts in the Street, many of them graduates of either Moody's or S.&P., make a good living spotting virtues in companies that the agencies overlooked and rated low. The idea is to pick out at low prices contenders whose ratings are likely to be upgraded. The other objective of independent analysis is to isolate companies whose ratings might be downgraded. Ratings have a major impact on price. The possibility of a downgrading is why the prudent investor ought not to stray beyond the A-rated fold. Going down a notch in quality will get you a higher return—but exposes you to more market risk. Top-rated companies like A.T.&T. and General Motors pay less for the money they borrow precisely because they are the cream of the crop.

Some of the risk in bonds is internal: a turn for the worse in the company's fortunes which might translate into a lower rating. Much of the risk is external. Bond prices move inversely with interest rates. If interest rates go up, prices go down. If rates go down, prices go up.

Let's take a look at that phenomenon. Most bonds trade in denominations of $1,000. A bond yielding 6 percent pays $60 a year, usually semi-annually. If interest rates rise, a company will have to pay more to borrow the capital it needs. It might have to come out with a 7 percent bond that returns $70 a year. If that happens, the older bond has to drop in price—probably to $859 from the original $1,000 because its fixed $60 a year payment is 7 percent of $859. The drop in market price is the only way the older bond can compete with the new higher yielding one.

The flip side of the coin is a decline in rates. Assume that newly issued bonds can be sold for 5 percent. The 6 percent bond will probably go to $1,200. It now has to pay only 5 percent to compete and its fixed $60 a year payment is 5 percent of $1,200. Bond rates are also shaped by the length of the loan. Investors who lend long term (20 or 30 years) can generally expect a higher return on their money because it is exposed to risk for a longer period than those who lend either intermediate (five to ten years), or short term (one or two years). Sometimes, however, the yield curve flattens, and the spread between long and short or intermediate bonds narrows. When that happens, it pays to stay short or intermediate.

The technical factors—rating and maturity—both spin on the axis of inflation and monetary policy. With inflation rising and monetary policy generally very tight, interest rates have also been rising. That means bond prices for the most part have been on the downgrade. Institutional investors have done all right in the long bear market in bonds because they tend to hang on to maturity. They can afford to do so. They have a continuous supply of fresh money coming in that gets put out at scaled up rates. Since most individual investors have neither of those luxuries going for them, their strategy is clear.

You avoid real or potential capital losses in a period of rising rates by buying short or intermediate bonds. The closer a bond is to maturity, the closer it trades to its $1,000 maturity value. In a period of declining rates, the strategy would be to go long. By doing so, you'd lock in a high return and at the same time hope to pick up a potential profit on the rise in prices.

All of this assumes, of course, that you are sensitive to swings in the interest cycle. You can get some insight into what's going on by watching the financial pages for changes in such barometers as the prime rate—the interest rate the banks charge their biggest and best customers. The Wall Street Journal, The New York Times, Forbes and Barron's are full of intelligent and useful commentary on the money and bond markets. They can give you the drift if not the precise wave on which the interest tide will turn.

That's all very well, you say. But what about those poor blokes who bought 20- or 30-year bonds back there in the early 'sixties when something like 4.35 percent looked very rich indeed? Then, when rates went bucketing right on up to better than 9 percent, they got the nice queasy feeling that always comes with having the value of an investment drop by half.

In general, bonds have been anything but a happy hedge against inflation. Adversity does have its uses, though. One widely employed strategy involves buying bonds that have fallen out of bed—in the argot of the Street, "discount" bonds. They trade below their $1,000 par value because the coupon interest they offer is lower than the return on newly issued maturities.

If you are planning for retirement, or to help finance your children's college education some 15 years from now, for example, you might be able to find bonds that will mature then, selling for 70 percent to 75 percent of their face value.

The strategy assumes that you are willing to settle for what may be comparatively modest current income as a trade-off against capital gains when the bonds mature. There is also the assumption that there will be no changes in the tax laws, and that the difference between the 75 cents on the dollar you paid for the bonds and the 100 cents on the dollar you get back will be subject to the lighter touch of the capital gains levy.

Conversely, people in search of high current income—retirees who need to piece out a pension, for example—benefited during this period of rising rates by concentrating on new issue bonds. The latter can be bought through brokers on a "net" basis, in effect without a commission because the company coming to market pays the selling costs. I am grateful to my *New York Times* colleague Robert Metz for the observation that there are advantages to sticking with new issue bonds slated for listing on the New York Stock Exchange rather than those earmarked for trading in the over-the-counter market.

The commission on listed bonds at this writing is generally $5. The market usually has enough depth so that the small buyer or seller can get a fair shake on the price. If you're trading over the counter, however, there are likely to be wide spreads between the buy and the sell side of the deal. The spread represents the dealer's profit, and you're the one who has to pay it.

If you stick with quality, realize that yield is a function of quality (the bigger the yield, the higher the risk), and have figured out when you'd like to get your money back, it's hard to get burned in the bond market. One caveat: check the call date on a bond before you buy. Corporate treasurers are as sensitive as litmus paper to swings in interest rates. There is hardly a financial man alive who doesn't go pink with pleasure at the prospect of redeeming a 10 percent bond if there's 7 percent money kicking around. Most bonds issued in the last decade or so have a built-in protection clause against redemption for the first five or ten years of their life. Even then, the call price carries a bit of sweetener as compensation for the lower rate at which you will be reinvesting the proceeds of the redemption.

As Merrill Lynch notes in "The Bond Book," however, a 38-page brochure available free at most of its branch offices, "When you buy existing bonds . . . you should consider what their first refunding price is in relation to the price you pay for them." The danger is that you might be paying a higher premium for the bond than the price at which it might be called away from you.

Another word about Treasuries and Federal agency bonds. They are just about the safest things around, and because of their low risk profile-yield less than corporates. You can check your local bank or the newspapers for details, but the Treasury sells one year notes every fourth Wednesday while two year notes are sold from the middle to the end of each month, depending on circumstances. All such sales are usually announced about a week beforehand. Four year notes are sold quarterly, toward the end of February, May, August and November. Five year notes and 15 year bonds are sold alternately each quarter, usually toward the end of December, March, June, and September.

The Treasury usually comes to market with a big package of securities early in February, May, August and November. The package varies, among other things, with the way the technicians want to stagger their maturities. There have been 10 year notes and 22 year bonds, 6¾ notes and a 29¾ year bond. Agency bonds such as those issued by the Federal Intermediate Credit Banks, Banks for Cooperatives, and the Federal Land Banks generally offer somewhat higher yields than Treasuries.

Some degree of diversification is as useful in bonds as in stocks, though the range need not be as broad. And diversification might be one reason for getting into the market through closed- or open-end bond funds rather than by direct investment.

Among the biggest closed-end bond funds you can track in the financial pages and Weisenberger (see Chapter 16), are American General Bond Fund, Drexel Bond-Debenture Trading Fund, John Hancock Investors, Inc., Montgomery Street Income Securities, and Mutual of Omaha Interest Shares. In all, there are 24 closed-end bond funds, most of which trade on the New York Stock Exchange.

Many of the closed-ends offer both good yields and often a way to buy bonds at a discount. The depth of the discounts varies with the state of the bond and stock markets. When both are down, the discounts deepen. The discounts also tend to vary with the portfolio quality. The conservatively managed American General Bond Fund, for instance, traded at a small premium for much of the period 1971-77, and then slipped to a small discount when interest rates seemed once again to be marching to historic highs. The fund has been upgrading a portfolio that was good to begin with. About 80 percent of assets were tucked into high quality debt, Government obligations, prime commercial paper and cash. The balance was a little more venturesome, but turnover was modest. All of that added up to a net asset value and a market price that moved pretty closely in train with each other.

Drexel Bond-Debenture, on the other hand, has sold at a discount of as much as 20 percent below asset value, partly because a good chunk of the portfolio has been in equities as well as bonds, and partly because the fund's aggressive approach to trading profits has made for very high portfolio turnover. Operating costs, as a result, tend to be comparatively high and cut into yield. Tom Herzfeld, probably the specialist in closed-ends, argues that "there's no point" in buying an open-end bond fund when "you can buy just as good a portfolio through a closed-end at a discount." There is some merit to that argument.

Many of the open-end bond funds carry an 8 percent load charge that can reduce a smaller investor's effective yield considerably. The industry trend is towards no-load. If it's maximum current income you want, my feeling is that you're better off with a no-load. Bond funds have different objectives. The Keystone group, for example, has one fund that specializes in investment grade bonds, another which specializes in medium growth bonds, and still another that specializes in discount bonds.

Many bond funds try to soup up their total return (income plus appreciation) with a blend of high-to-medium and low grade bonds. Others shoot the moon with "junk" bonds, low grade deep-discount bonds. That category includes the Lord Abbett Bond-Debenture Fund, Keystone B-4, and the First Investors Fund for Income, among others. All such funds are riskier than their more conservative fellows, but they have proved extremely popular—as popular as the stream of direct junk underwritings yielding 12 percent and 13 percent that have lately been coming to market in heavy volume.

The junk bond funds are "performance" oriented, selling bonds when they go up in price, and rolling over the proceeds into still more high yielding junk. All of that trading costs money, but junk bond fund managers insist they minimize risks by carefully researching the situations they move in and out of. "We research these bonds and we are very careful," R. Patterson Warlick, portfolio manager for the Lord Abbett Bond-Debenture Fund, told *Forbes* recently. "We use (Standard & Poor's) ratings only to understand what others are likely to do."

Many income funds managers, including the junkmen, have definitely done better than the major stock market averages over the last several years. Many have also definitely done better than most small investors could have done for themselves. As with stock funds, however, the moral is clear: you have to be certain about your own objectives, and you have to do enough homework to establish that the performance figures you're looking at aren't just a flash in the pan.

You have to think about flashes in the pan because Wall Street is all evanescence—a big scale packaging operation that will sell you growth stocks when they are in vogue, bonds when they seem to be the rage, and anything else in between. None of the packaging is plain brown wrapper stuff. It's designed to generate profits: the load charge and management fees on the open-end funds; smaller front-end load charges and sometimes what are in effect redemption costs on the so-called unit trusts.

Some unit trusts specialize in corporate bonds,

others in tax-exempts. The latter are by far the biggest market, but unit trusts crop up frequently enough in the taxable income field to be examined here.

The trusts are fixed pools of securities selected and underwritten by a clutch of big firms that includes Bache Halsey Stuart Shields, Inc., and Merrill Lynch, Pierce, Fenner & Smith, Inc. The units representing a share in the pool are generally sold at $1,000 apiece, plus sales commissions ranging from 2.5 percent to 4.5 percent. Besides the sales commissions, the sponsors sometimes profit on the spread between the price at which they've bought debt obligations and the price at which those same securities are sold to the trust. Many of the securities that wind up in the trust, in fact, are obligations that the sponsors help to underwrite. Thus, the trusts sometimes offer the sponsors an additional outlet for debt securities they might otherwise have had to sell at lower prices through ordinary underwriting channels.

Unlike the mutual funds, the unit trusts charge no advisory fees. They are unmanaged, so constructed as to pick off the best yields prevailing at the moment they are put together, consistent with safety. The mutual funds, on the other hand, are managed. Their objective is to maximize whatever gains can be made on swings in the market.

A lot of thought goes into the blending of the 20 to 30 or so different issues that might be put into a trust portfolio. Many trusts say they will not go for anything less than an A rating. In practice, though, they often pick up lower medium grade issues that in their opinion should be rated a notch higher by Standard &

Poor's or Moody's. The portfolio pickers throw in a pinch of this and a pinch of that to come up with the richest overall yield they can find. They might average a group of A-rated utilities, for example, with the higher returns available on foreign bonds, or private placement securities for which there are no ready markets.

The trick to the blending is to produce a yield that looks good at the moment the trust is being sold. The risk from the buyer's side is always that yields might go higher still, leaving him locked into an investment whose value has slipped below his purchase price. Consider the unhappy plight of people who bought unit trusts yielding 4 percent a decade ago. They've been double-teamed. Their returns are very low against the backdrop of today's rates, and they've got sizable paper losses on their portfolios. On the other hand, people who bought unit trusts at 9 percent or more are feeling very comfortable indeed.

Short of a default on some portfolio issue, investors get back the full $1,000 per unit when the trust breaks up. Most sponsors stand ready to redeem units before the breakup. Some will do so only at the lower bid side of the underlying bonds, some will give you the full offer price. In either case, the redemption price reflects what's happening in the market. It could be higher than your purchase price; it could be lower. The risk factor is the reason why anyone who buys a unit trust should be certain that he's got a big enough cash reserve to hang in there, if need be, until the trust matures.

The same observation can be made of income-oriented mutual funds, of course. Which to buy? If rates are high, a unit trust might be useful for people who are nearing or already in retirement. For those with shorter term investment objectives—a down payment on a house, or financing college bills, for example—a well-managed mutual fund might be a better alternative.

Many income funds salt their portfolio mix with convertible bonds, a hybrid that sports some of the features of both stocks and bonds. As the name suggests, convertible bonds (and preferreds) can be exchanged for a fixed number of common shares at a specific price. That's a worthwhile privilege to have if the stock suddenly takes off beyond the conversion price. While you're waiting for the frog to turn into a prince, you've got a bond—a bond which because of the conversion feature generally offers a lower rate of interest than straight senior securities. As we noted about preferred stocks, there are two ways to win, and two ways to lose. If stock prices go up and/or interest rates decline, the price of the bond will rise. If stock prices go down and/or interest rates rise, the price of the bond will decline.

There are some compensations. Convertibles generally carry less risk than common stock. If the underlying common stock sells off, a convertible generally trades at "investment" value. There is a floor under the bond when its yield approaches prevailing interest rates. Convertibles offer somewhat more capital gains potential than straight bonds, but they really have to be analyzed in terms of the common stock. If you think the stock market is going off on a great binge but want to hedge your bets, a convertible might be the way to go.

TOP DOLLAR TIPS

(1) Check points on corporate bonds: Do profits cover interest charges by a good margin? How much debt does the company have outstanding? Are the bonds of at least upper medium investment quality?

(2) The best time to buy bonds in the secondary market is when interest rates are rising and prices declining.

(3) The best time to buy new issue bonds is when interest rates are rising.

(4) If you want the diversification of a mutual fund that specializes in bonds, why not consider a closed-end bond fund trading at a discount.

Chapter 21

COLLECTIBLES

There are times when the acquisitive itch seems to have turned the U.S. into one great big magpie's nest. People are trading and collecting almost anything that has a bit of flash to it—brass buttons, gold coins, empty whiskey bottles, old electric trains, comic books, matchbooks, plates, first editions, tintypes and maybe even chamber pots, for all I know.

A lot of that is fun, but scratch a collector and underneath you are likely to find a robber baron on the make. Put the squeeze on a small corner of scarce goods, the reasoning goes, and the world will beat a path to your door. Look at the sedulously promoted romance of collectibles, gold coins and graphics.

With inflation running roughshod over anyone who works for a salary, the pitch to the pocketbook nerve need not be too subtle.

The people who merchandise the Krugerrand, for example, are beating the drum for the South African gold coin as a "unique" form of protection against "fluctuating currencies and high inflation." Associated American Artists, one of the best known names in graphics, titillates potential clients with the assertion that "many of (our) original prints . . . have increased in value as much as sixty times."

The merchandisers are working the seam of Calvinism that twists through the American soul. Collecting things may be fun, but it has to be profitable, too. Gold has a mystique all its own, particularly among conservatives who look on the yellow metal as the last line of defense against the systematic debauching of the world's currencies. There are lots of ways to own gold, but all of them entail taking on a substantial amount of risk. Like any other kind of commodities market, gold is dominated by professionals and there is very little warmth in the metal to temper the sheared sheep.

Consider the speculative frenzy that pushed gold from $35 an ounce to $197.50 an ounce on Dec. 30, 1974—the day before it became legal for Americans to own gold bullion for the first time in 41 years. Though subjected to some very heavy drum beating, Americans just didn't go out and snap up the yellow stuff in the manic way speculators had hoped to see. The goldbugs, many of them untutored nonprofessionals, were whipsawed when prices subsequently sold off to $106.60 an ounce. That was in August 1976. Prices had plummeted to the lowest level in three years.

It was another long two years before gold got back up to $200 an ounce, a happening that was attributed to the deterioration of the dollar against other currencies. In their own clinical way, the pros refer to the deep sell-off that began in 1975 as a "correction." It would be unrealistic to suppose that there will not be many more corrections ahead—corrections in which gold will once again prove to be a negative inflation hedge.

One of the problems with gold is the cost of owning it. In bullion form, the stuff has to be assayed, stored and insured. It produces no income and has to be regarded as strictly a make-or-break market play. My own feeling is that bullion is for the big boys. But if you think Armageddon is just down the pike and you're convinced that owning some gold is a prudent long term hedge, gold certificates are an easy way to get into the game.

The certificates are sold by Deak & Co. (1800 K St., N.W., Washington D.C. 20006), Dreyfus Gold Deposits, Inc. (600 Madison Ave., New York, N.Y. 10022) and many other brokerage firms. A minimum investment of $2,500 gets you an "undivided but specific" interest in an identifiable bar of bullion, bought with the pooled buying power of other goldbugs. Most firms charge a 3 percent commission on the buy side. The load on the sell side ranges from 1 percent to 3 percent. There are storage and insurance charges to boot. Thus, taking only the round trip buy and sell costs into account, gold will have to go up at least 4 percent and maybe 6 percent before you begin to break even.

Similar front- and back-end loads make investing in gold coins like the Krugerrand a tough struggle to break even, too. The Krugerrand contains exactly one troy ounce of gold. It is sold not for its numismatic value—as a collector's item—but as a convenient way to hold the yellow metal. Because the Krugerrand contains exactly one ounce of gold, the value of the coin can be checked against the daily closing price of the metal in most newspapers.

Prices on the Krugerrand itself tend to vary widely. A recent spot check showed a difference of almost $3 between two major New York City dealers on the purchase price for one coin. Their price on ten coins was identical. It's possible to buy the Krugerrand by mail from dealers in states that have low sales taxes. In high tax areas such as New York City, however, you have to add the 8 percent sales levy—an impost that adds considerably to the built-in premium over the world price at which the South African and most other gold coins retail.

A big part of the premium comes from the mark-ups linked into the chain of distribution. The South African mint sells the Krugerrand to wholesalers at the world price of gold, plus 3 percent. Shipping and interest charges tack on another six-tenths of 1 percent. By the time the wholesalers and retailers have added their profits on top, you might need a gain of $12 or $13—not counting sales taxes—to break even on the deal.

But breaking even on paper is one thing. In the real world it is something else again. The spreads between the price at which dealers sell gold coins and the price at which they are willing to buy them back may be as much as $3 or $4, again not counting local taxes.

In terms of cost, probably the cheapest way to get into the yellow metal is by purchasing gold stocks, which tend to yo-yo more or less in sympathy with the world price of the stuff. The risks are the same, but straight out brokerage commissions are lower than the sales load on gold certificates and lower than the mark-ups and price spreads on coins.

Furthermore, stocks at least generate current dividend income, while gold in any other form does not. If you're waiting to cash in on a big turn in the market, you might just as well have something coming in while you wait.

The yield on the so-called Kaffirs, in fact, those South African gold stocks with such tongue-twisting names as East Driefontein Gold Mining, Hartobeestfontein Gold Mining and Kloof Gold Mining, tend to be rather high. They are high partly because the South African mines have traditionally paid out a larger proportion of their earnings in dividends, partly because South Africa's racial and diplomatic problems have been factored into the price of Kaffirs. Because they carry so much risk, even the most intrepid goldbugs opt for diversification. One way to buy into a bundle of South African gold stocks is through ASA, Ltd., a closed-end investment company traded on the New York Stock Exchange.

Kaffirs at this writing account for almost 80 percent of ASA's portfolio. The stock is so hotly pursued by goldbugs that ASA, unlike most closed-end investment companies, has traditionally sold at a premium—and often a very high premium—over net asset value.

Much of the money pouring into gold and collectibles seems to be coming from disenchanted bulls. "Some of the people who took a beating in the stock market," says Alfred M. Isselbacher, who owns the Isselbacher Gallery in New York City, "are investing in art for appreciation."

There are almost as many success stories about collectibles as there are about those lucky folks in Rochester who 70 years ago bought into the Haloid Company at $3 a share before it metamorphosed into the Xerox Corporation. Feature editors gobble up such snippets as how Action Comics No. 1, the June 1938 issue in which Superman and Clark Kent burst on an unsuspecting world, sells for $4,500—quite a return on an initial investment of 10 cents.

There are gee whiz anecdotes in every field, such as the New Jersey sales consultant's seemingly undistinguished heirloom which, on closer inspection, turned out to be a fourteenth-century Italian work that was ultimately auctioned for $55,000. For the diamond bugs, there is the word that prices of top quality gems have nearly tripled since 1970.

There is no question that quality artifacts of one kind or another have appreciated handsomely. Equally, however, a lot of the tub-thumping comes from people with vested interests in success stories. As *Forbes* recently noted, "There are auction houses selling diamonds from 'famous estates,' mail-order firms hawking raw diamonds by the bag from 'world famous South African mines,' fly-by-night telephone boiler-room operators selling them by the box; California commodity brokers designing a diamonds mutual fund."

There are humbugs everywhere. The world of collectibles is in many respects very much like the world of Wall Street. Markets go up, they go down, and sometimes they don't move at all. In the 1974 recession, for example, even works by such well-known names as Léger and Utrillo were marked down anywhere from 10 percent to 60 percent. There was a big break in the retail diamond market between 1962 and 1965 when prices on better stones were cut by 25 percent or more. And like many big ticket paintings and other collectibles, diamonds also took a pasting in 1974-75.

Book collectors also know that no tree goes to the sky. As H.J. Maidenberg, himself a collector of rare distinction, recently noted in *The New York Times*, some price shifts are seemingly "inexplicable." Take the case of Edward S. Curtis' massive work, *The North American Indian*. The 40 volume set, half of which consists of illustrations, was published between 1907 and 1930. The full set sold for $20,000 in 1972 and was auctioned for $60,000 five years later. Recently the price backed off to $50,000 and is probably headed even lower.

How come? "Either the sharp rise in price pushed the volume out of the reach of collectors, or it flushed out a number of other copies from collections, lowering the set's value by increasing the supply," reported Mr. Maidenberg.

The prices on some objects never move at all because there is no market for them. A couple of years ago, for example, I bought a couple of modestly priced lithographs from Associated American Artists. Did Sylvan Cole think they would appreciate? "No dice," the A.A.A. president said bluntly. When you buy graphics done by unknowns, "you are getting your profit by enjoying the work."

If your goal is profit before enjoyment, you are probably safest in sticking to quality. As *ARTnewsletter's* informative brochure "Investors Guide to the Art Market" (122 E. 42nd St., New York, N.Y. 10017) notes, there are two other considerations to take into account: Is the supply of the item limited, and is demand likely to continue strong?

"A limited supply," the *ARTnews* editors observe, "insures that additional items cannot flood the market and decrease the value of your investment." As to demand, that's a value judgment that has to be made on the basis of expert knowledge "of the particular work and its relationship to similar items."

There are no guarantees, the editors continue, "but an emphasis on quality when the piece is purchased . . . can weigh the odds in your favor if you . . . have to sell during an economic recession." The big problem with collectibles of almost every kind is the lack of liquid secondary markets. You can't sell an old stamp or an undistinguished litho with anything like the ease with which you can unload 100 shares of Telephone.

For serious collectors the lack of liquidity almost invariably means working with a dealer, or even several of them. Finding a good dealer is like trying to find a good stockbroker—it takes effort. Word of mouth is as reliable a guide as any, but as Sylvan Cole notes there is no substitute for legwork and homework.

"You definitely have to make the rounds of the dealers, see everything in sight, and get all the lectures you can," he says. That advice holds true for every variety of collectible. Some other hints from the experts:

● Concentrate on one area. "The sum is far, far greater than the parts," says Peter T. Kraus, president of Ursus Books, Ltd., dealers in rare literary materials. "The value is in collections, the more complete, the better. Builders of collections rarely come out losers."

● Shop as many auctions as you can, and hone your judgment to a fine edge by keeping precise notes on prices. Prepare for an auction as you would for any business deal. Look the material over carefully before the sale, check out price estimates, identify what you want to bid on, figure out your own bid price and don't budge from it.

● Get plugged into trade magazines, associations and other resources. If books seem to be your meat, for example, the trader's bible is the *AB Bookman's*

Weekly (P.O. Box AB, Clifton, N.J. 07015). For antiquarians there are such publications as *Antiques* (551 Fifth Ave., New York, N.Y. 10017), and *Antique Monthly* (P.O. Drawer 2, Tuscaloosa, Ala. 35401). For coin collectors there is the "red book," *A Guide Book of United States Coins and the American Numismatic Association* (P.O. Box 2366, Colorado Springs, Colo. 80901). In short, there are resources for every taste. Just make sure that what you buy suits your fancy. You may have to live with it for a long, long time.

TOP DOLLAR TIPS

(1) The gold market is for professionals. What makes you think you can beat them at their own game?

(2) If you think you ought to be in gold, the best way is through the stock market. Stocks, at least, generate some income. Gold bars don't.

(3) Gold coins—like most collectibles—are sold at very wide price spreads. The spreads mean that over the short run it's often impossible to sell at as good a price as you bought.

(4) If you are a collector, make sure you like what you buy. You may have to live with the purchase.

HOW TO MANAGE YOUR INCOME TAX

Chapter 22

TAX-EXEMPT BONDS

It's easy to understand the dynamics behind the big boom in tax-exempt municipal bonds, and why, for many investors, they have become the chosen instrument in the never-ending fight against the tax collector.

Take the case of a couple that was making $18,000 a year a decade ago. Now they are making $36,000. Their income has doubled, but because of inflation their true purchasing power has barely budged. At the same time, the couple's incremental tax rate on a joint return—what they have to pay on the next dollar they earn—has jumped from 28 percent to 45 percent. In that bracket, according to figures compiled by Fidelity Management & Research Co., a tax-free 5.5 percent yield is the equivalent of a 10 percent taxable yield. Since a safe, dependable long term investment paying 10 percent is difficult to find anywhere except in a mortgage, tax-exempts get the nod.

Safety and dependability are supposed to be the hallmarks of the tax-exempt bonds issued by states, their agencies and municipalities. The near-bankruptcy of New York City, however, and the epic struggle it took to resuscitate the moribund New York State Urban Development Corp. underscored the fact that solid-seeming investment grade issues are not always what they are cracked up to be. Municipal bonds are rated in the same way as corporate bonds, but the lack of early warning signals on the New York situation called the credibility of the rating agencies into question. The moral is clear. There is as much risk in tax-exempts as in any other security.

The variety is huge. Broadly, tax-exempts break down into two major categories, general obligations ("G.O.'s" in the argot) and revenue bonds. The former are secured by local government's unlimited tax powers; the latter by an earmarked source of revenue—tolls from a bridge, say, or rents from a housing project.

General obligations are still the best credit risk, but their credibility was also called into question by the New York debacle. Revenue bonds tend to carry somewhat higher yields than G.O.'s, but the return is a function of the overall credit rating and how secure the source of revenue is. The New Jersey Sports & Exposition Authority's 7.5 percent revenue bonds originally scheduled to mature in the year 2009, for example, were rated low. They sold at a deep discount until the throngs which spilled through the turnstiles demonstrated that big time horse racing could flourish in the New Jersey meadowlands.

Some shrewd buyers turned some very handsome capital gains on the Sports Authority bonds. Capital gains are nice at any time, but it's important to remember that only the interest on municipals is tax-free. Capital gains are not. There is another kicker to consider, though. Bonds issued within a state are exempt from the payment of state and local taxes there. Puerto Rican bonds get even more special treatment. They are exempt from state and local levies everywhere.

The shelter against state and local levies can make for a significantly better return in such high tax states as New York, Massachusetts, and Pennsylvania. That's the reason why many municipal bond mutual funds tend to load up with securities from those states. Doing so makes them more attractive to investors in such major money centers as New York, Boston and Philadelphia.

Rage against the depredation of the income tax has made it easy to sell municipals. The rage often blinds some investors to the fact they ought not to be in tax-exempts at all. Check your income tax return, talk to your accountant. What tax bracket are you in? Unless you're in the 35 percent and up bracket, you can probably get a higher net return in some other form of investment. Because of the tax feature, tax-exempts generally yield less than Governments or corporates.

You have to look at munis in terms of both your tax bracket and the entire spectrum of interest rates. Then, ask yourself what the bottom line is. You might be better off in Governments or high grade corporate bonds.

For the small investor, munis carry some of the same trading disadvantages as corporates. Tax-exempts are usually issued in denominations of $1,000 or multiples of $5,000. In general, anything under $10,000 is considered an odd lot. Buying or selling bond odd lots almost invariably means that you pay a penalty on the price spreads. The penalty may be a good reason for not trying to diversify into several muni issues if you've got only a modest amount of cash to put to work. "It is better to hold a large amount of one high-quality issue than smaller quantities of several bonds," says Tom Holt, head of the Holt Investment Advisory.

Questions of liquidity aside, there may be some circumstances under which you'd want to think twice about owning tax-exempts. If your income fluctuates widely, the tax exemption might be helpful one year and do nothing whatever for you the next. It also helps to remember that you cannot try to put a double squeeze on the I.R.S. by borrowing money to buy tax-exempts. The idea is that you can't benefit twice—once by taking a deduction on interest payments on the loan, and again by the tax-free flow of interest payments from the munis.

I.R.S. policing in the area is tight, and ambiguities can get you into trouble. Hence, if you do a fair amount of borrowing on a regular basis—perhaps to exercise stock options—prudence might dictate that you stay away from munis. Even with a meticulous set of records you might not be able to demonstrate to the I.R.S. satisfaction that you have not been borrowing to buy munis.

One of the most common mistakes muni buyers make is to chase yields. The bigger they are, the better they are, the reasoning goes. Not so with munis any more than with any other kind of security. The important question to ask, says Philip W. Goldsmith, head of municipal research at Prescott, Ball & Turben, is "how come the yield is at that level?" "The onus," the Prescott, Ball partner continues, "should be on the salesman and his research people to explain the why of the yield."

For the most part, yields—and prices—are shaped by agency ratings. In some cases, though, argues Mr. Goldsmith, the ratings are too high. In others, they are too low.

Is an area gaining or losing industry? Who are the big taxpayers and how are they making out? How much debt does the municipality have outstanding and what is its ability to service that debt?

These are standard analytical questions. The rating agencies raise them all the time, but it doesn't hurt an investor to pose them, too. The agencies don't have a monopoly on truth. Besides, much of what goes into the rating game is judgmental. Asking the right questions can help you penetrate the fog of salesmanship that obscures so many municipal offerings.

A lot of the salesmanship goes into muni bond mutual funds and muni bond unit trusts. The bond funds alone have total assets of better than $3 billion, while big underwriters like Merrill Lynch, and John Nuveen & Co., have been stamping out unit trusts like so many busy cookie cutters. There is brisk competition between the two wings of the industry, just as in corporate bonds, and the difficulty of making a choice is compounded by the load—no load question.

Most of the load muni funds are "low load." The Kemper Municipal Bond Fund, for example, charges a 4.75 percent sales commission, compared with the 8 percent that is common on many straight income funds. No-loads, however, have carved out a broad beachhead in the muni market. Many of the no-loads, in fact, are managed by organizations that have traditionally levied a sales fee on the other open-ends they handle.

Among the very biggest muni funds (Fidelity Municipal Bond Fund, Dreyfus Tax Exempt, Kemper Municipal Bond Fund, Rowe Price Tax Free Income Fund, Fidelity Limited Term Municipals, and Scudder Managed Municipals), only Kemper charges a sales fee. The weight in that line-up suggests that some of the best promotion heads in the industry have decided that loads are just not salable to sophisticated income-oriented investors. And people who buy muni bond funds seem to be both better-heeled and more knowledgeable than mutual fund investors as a group. The average ticket, or sale, is higher with muni funds, and industry surveys suggest that muni fund investors have had at least some exposure to other securities.

They are sophisticated enough to realize that load

charges can cut seriously into yield. And yield, of course, is an important element to look at when you're weighing the purchase of one muni fund against another. It is, however, not the only thing to pull out of the fine print in the prospectus. Compare management costs, the ratings and kind of bonds that have been put into the portfolio, the geographic spread on the bonds.

You may just find, for example, that Fund A is able to offer a comparatively high yield because its portfolio is jammed with low rated Baa bonds—a risk that you just might not want to take. Or you might find that Fund B is loaded with securities from industrial eastern states whose finances tend to be on the shaky side—again a risk that you just might not want to accept. The funds sell diversification, of course. The argument is that reaching down the quality scale for yield is safe enough when the risk is spread over a bundle of many different issues.

The logic of that argument seems convincing enough when things are going well, but it doesn't always work in a declining market—as many muni fund managers found to their distress recently. When interest rates started to rise and prices began to slide, so did muni fund asset values. The managers tried to negotiate the tricky turn in the market by doing the obvious things. They shortened their maturities and moved into cash so as to be able to meet a flood of redemptions—the first since the Tax Reform Act of 1976 made it possible for the muni bond funds to operate.

It was a bad time for the funds, one of which advertises "Tax-Free Income Without Going Out on a Limb." There are no free rides in Wall Street, as the performance figures on the muni bond (and all other funds) demonstrate.

Where to check the performance figures? The prospectus is the first piece of raw material to mine. Most of the big no-load mutual funds advertise in newspaper financial pages and in magazines like *Barron's*, *Forbes* and *Money*. Most also have toll-free telephones, and will mail out a prospectus on request. Other resources include Yale Hirsch's *Mutual Fund Almanac* and Weisenberger (See Chapter 16).

Most unit trust sponsors do a fair amount of advertising, too. Their prospectuses are also must reading. Everything we've said about straight bond unit trusts applies to muni bond unit trusts. The muni bond funds are fixed, unmanaged pools of capital that generally carry an up-front entry fee of 3 percent to 4.5 percent. Many portfolios become the final resting place for bonds the sponsors could not—or would not—move through regular distribution channels.

Like the funds, the trusts are sold in units of $1,000. They offer diversification and a predictable rate of return over the maturity of the trust, which may range from as little as five years on out to 30 years. Because the unit sponsors sell yield, portfolio quality may not be as solid as you would like, and there are definite liquidity problems. If you have to sell before the trust breaks up, you may take a beating on price. The trusts are only for long haul investors with solid cash reserves, and even then only if the return is right.

TOP DOLLAR TIPS

(1) You can't borrow money to buy tax-exempts, and only the interest on municipals is tax-free. Capital gains are not.

(2) Check your tax bracket. If you're not in the 35 percent range, you might be able to get higher net yields in Governments or corporates.

(3) Odd lot muni buyers can get hurt on price spreads. If you've got only a modest amount of cash to work with, buy only one issue instead of trying to diversify.

(4) For diversification, consider a mutual fund or a unit trust.

Chapter 23

TAX
SHELTERS

The line between tax avoidance and tax evasion is clear enough. It's the difference between having a couple of extra cents to jingle in your pocket after the I.R.S. has taken its cut, and scoffing your mashed potatoes off a stainless steel tray at Danbury or some other country club run by the Feds.

Tax avoidance is big business. Brokerage firms, some tax lawyers, finders and an assortment of other fixers are all jostling one another for a slice of the market. And what a market it is—so big that no one has a handle on all of the numbers. The best estimate is that participations in one kind of tax shelter or other—oil and gas drilling programs, real estate syndications, and even railroad car leasing deals—are being sold at the rate of better than $2 billion a year.

Tax shelters are entirely legal loopholes that have been drilled through the Internal Revenue code by such shrewd, hardworking special interests as the oil and gas, farming, and real estate lobbies. The rationale is that the shelters help to channel capital into major corners of the economy.

The incentives from the point of view of people who sell tax shelters are high. Up-front sales commissions can range anywhere from 6 percent to 8.5 percent of the amount of cash invested. Depending on how the deal is structured, the insiders can also be pulling down handsome management fees, expenses, and a very sizable chunk of the profits—if any.

That is not to say that good management isn't worth its salt. It is to say that one of the most common structures shelters take—the limited partnership—can be booby trapped with all sorts of potential conflicts of interest. There are other risks as well, about which more later. As always, you have to weigh those risks in terms of potential reward. The objective is to turn cash that would otherwise go to the I.R.S. into outright tax savings, tax-sheltered income, or lightly taxed capital gains.

Unfortunately, not all of those objectives can be maximized at the same time. Tax shelters are a very tricky business. Why get into something so tricky when the relatively less complicated world of municipal bonds can offer some of the same advantages?

Tax shelter net yields, for one thing, are sometimes higher than can be got in munis. And for another, the odds on coming away with a capital gain are sometimes higher. The prospect that an investment in good commercial real estate might be worth more money 10 years down the road is not such a bad bet. It's probably a better bet than a hazard on the imponderables of what the muni bond market will be doing 10 years out.

The same people who sell muni bonds will be more than happy to sell you tax shelters, too. Almost every major brokerage firm has jumped into the business with both feet. Back in 1975, the ubiquitous Merrill Lynch, for example, sold about $50 million in tax shelter equity investments. Today the figure is well over the $100 million mark.

There are two kinds of tax shelters—public offerings registered with the Securities & Exchange Commission, and state regulatory agencies and private placements limited to 35 or fewer investors. The latter need not be registered with the S.E.C.. The public offerings generally require minimum investments of $5,000. They are usually tailored to people of comparatively modest means. Merrill Lynch, for instance, has sold a whole series of participations in existing commercial real estate. Investors had to sign a "suitability" statement indicating a minimum gross annual income of $20,000 and a net worth of $20,000 (excluding home and furnishings), or a net worth (again excluding home and furnishings) of $75,000.

Private placements, on the other hand, invariably require higher minimum investments and a more stringent assets test. On a farm land deal that Merrill Lynch placed with 30 investors, for example, the minimum buy was one participation at $42,400. The 30 investors had to show a net worth of more than $150,000 (exclusive of home, home furnishings and automobiles) and a minimum gross income for Federal income tax purposes of $60,000.

The difference in arithmetic is rooted in the tax laws. If you are allowed to get only 35 people in on a deal, you need a correspondingly heavy commitment to handle anything of any size. The asset test is also partly a function of risk. Tax shelters are only for long term investors. Don't get in over your head. Secondary markets are extremely limited, and in many cases non-existent. You must have enough of a financial cushion to be able to hang on until the shelter liquidates. Tax shelters ought not to be bought with money that's been earmarked for the kids' college or for your own retirement. The risk-reward ratio is so heavily weighted on the risk side that I don't think it makes much sense to get into a shelter unless you've got a big chunk of income in the 50 percent tax bracket. Even then you've got to be careful about going whole hog. Executive financial counselors such as the Bank of America's Peter Mazonas suggest that no more than 25 percent of your discretionary investment capital should be socked into tax shelters.

Investing in a pool of capital used to acquire existing commercial real estate is one of the most conservative approaches to tax shelter. Samplings by Merrill Lynch on several such deals it has sponsored show that about 70 percent of the people who bought them grossed between $20,000 and $50,000 a year. Some 65 percent of the purchasers reported net worths of between $75,000 and $300,000. Most (about 65 percent) were either professionals, executives or owned their own businesses. A surprisingly high proportion (about 25 percent) identified themselves as either retired persons or housewives.

The typical real estate deal, like most shelters, is a three-legged stool otherwise known as a limited partnership. The limited or silent partners have no voice in the day-to-day operations of the venture. They put up the bulk of the capital. The general partner usually, but not always, also puts up some capital. It is the latter's job to make the investments, keep the books, and distribute the profits—if any. The third leg is the manager, generally paid on a fee basis for running things. The manager, often, is a corporate offshoot of the general partner.

The tax deductible items in real estate are familiar enough—taxes, maintenance, interest payments and depreciation on the cost value of the buildings. The income, of course, is from rentals. Most such deals are structured to yield the limited partners a tax-free 7 percent to 8 percent a year, and the prospect of capital gains when the buildings are sold as the depreciation on them runs down. There are usually some up-front deductions that can be written off against other income, but they tend to be modest in comparison with other types of real estate investments—Government-subsidized housing, for example.

The deductions on existing real estate are also very modest in comparison with the great crap shoot of oil and gas drilling programs, where a limited partner can usually count on a 70 percent to 90 percent write-off against his investment in the first year. The write-off is generated by the pass-through of selling expenses, administrative expenses and deductions for such intangible drilling costs as labor, fuel and repairs.

The drilling game also holds out the prospect of partially tax-sheltered income from any well that hits. If you've got a lot of money in the 50 percent bracket, enough to make Uncle Sam an omnipresence, the game may be worth the candle. "Wildcat" or exploratory programs are at absolutely the riskiest edge of the spectrum. "Development" programs based on wildcat finds are only slightly less risky.

The entrepreneurial types who sell development programs insist it is "rational" for the investor who lucks into production to get his money back in four years or so, exclusive of tax benefits; and to reap a 2-to-1 return on his cash over the normal 10-year life of a producing well. There are, of course, no guarantees. Dry holes are the rule. Only one wildcat in 10 hits a new field, and only one out of every 40 or 50 turns out to be a significant commercial success. Every producing well is not a profitable well.

The fact that you can hit oil and still not break into the profits column is a reminder that every tax shelter has to stand on its own two feet. If the basic economics are not right, the fanciest tax savings in the world are not going to help. Scrape off all of the Béarnaise, and you've still got horsemeat.

Even an investment in something so conservative-seeming as office buildings still has to meet some basic tests. Can you be sure that the neighborhood won't change? Will the partnership be able to attract and hang on to solid tenants? Is the structure of the deal sound enough to absorb rising taxes, escalating operating costs and still turn a profit? Interested in taking a shot at cattle feeding? Then you've got to be aware that beef prices bucket all over the lot and mindful that hundreds of operators got wiped out in the great bear market of 1974.

Want to make your tax-deferred fortune in something so exotic as railroad car leasing? Can you be sure that demand for boxcars will continue at the high level of the last few years? Are per diem and mileage rates on the car going to be high enough to cover your interest costs, and other fixed charges?

They may seem like obvious questions, but you need something to help neutralize the high pressure selling. Take a hint from William G. Brennan, whose *Brennan Reports* (817 Carnegie Ave., P.O. Box 357, Johnstown, Pa. 15907) is one of the most authoritative sources in the business. He notes that promoters frequently strain both "imagination and tax law" in order to hustle "multiple-write-off shelters."

One of the biggest risks, in fact, is that the promoters have either misunderstood or misinterpreted the tax laws to the point where you may be buying not a shelter but a mincing machine. It might well be that the Internal Revenue Service might disallow deductions a hapless limited partner has been taking, either because they weren't kosher in the first place or because of changes in the tax laws. The money you thought you were sheltering could be subject to recapture and a nightmare list of penalties. Don't move without first asking your accountant to check out the tax angles for you.

Bill Brennan ticks off a number of other points that should be explored:

- The Sponsor's Background. How long has he been in business and how well did his other programs work out? If he's a Johnny-come-lately with no track record, pass him by.

- The Track Record. Most prospectuses and private placement memoranda are chock-a-block with performance figures on the sponsor's previous offerings. Usually there is a "Limited Partners' Payout Table" that lists revenues and operating costs attributable to the limited partners. There should be a good amount of daylight between those two figures. "If after six years prior programs have not produced revenues sufficient to have paid expenses," cautions Mr. Brennan, "a serious question exists as to the program's feasibility." *Caveat emptor.*

- Management Fees. In oil and gas drilling programs, they ought not to exceed 4 percent to 5 percent of the proceeds. If the fees are higher than that, notes Mr. Brennan, the general partner ought to be taking on some unusual expenses—brokerage commissions, for example. Every dollar that gets siphoned off up front is one less dollar working for you.

- Revenue Sharing. How much cash is the general partner himself putting into the deal? If he doesn't have any money at all at risk, his share of the revenues should be small until the limited partners have got all of their original capital back, plus a reasonable return.

- Liquidity. Does the general partner stand willing to redeem limited partnership interests after the program has been in business for a couple of years? How fair are the terms under which he stands willing to do so?

- Assessability. Can you be hit for additional capital contributions if the cost estimates go awry? Can you be penalized if you are unable—or unwilling—to come up with additional capital?

TOP DOLLAR TIPS

(1) Unless you've got a big chunk of money in the 50 percent bracket, think twice about getting into a tax shelter.

(2) Tax shelters are fraught with potential conflicts of interest between the managing partner and limited partners. Make sure you know who gets what.

(3) Shelter investments must dovetail with your overall tax situation. Lack of coordination can actually increase rather than minimize your tax liability. Check things out with your accountant.

(4) Tax shelters are only part of the investment picture. Limit them to 25 percent of your portfolio.

Chapter 24

DEALING WITH THE I.R.S.

The Internal Revenue code runs to about 6,000 pages of fine print and is shot through with contradictions. If your 10-year-old son has a severe malocclusion and your dentist recommends that he take up the clarinet to improve his bite, both the instrument and the cost of the lessons are tax deductible. On the other hand, you can't write off the cost of a toothbrush or toothpaste. The cost of belonging to Alcoholics Anonymous is tax-deductible, and you can deduct the fees of your favorite acupuncturist, but you can't take depreciation on an automobile bought entirely for medical reasons.

Somehow almost every effort to simplify the

patchwork of law and interpretation only makes it more of a crazy quilt. As Haskins & Sells, one of the Big Eight accounting firms recently told its clients, the increasing complexity of the code has made "tax relief . . . more elusive."

"These complexities and frequent changes in tax laws make tax planning more essential than ever before and have increased the cost of failing to plan," said Haskins & Sells.

Really effective tax planning takes: (a) a basic understanding of the tax rules; (b) well-defined financial goals; (c) up-to-date information; (d) and a sense of timing.

No matter how disheveled the state of the law, advance planning is a must. You will always pay less tax if your income is spread more or less evenly over two years than if a big chunk of it is lumped into one year.

As Prentice-Hall, Inc. (Englewood Cliffs, N.J. 07632) notes in its Executive Action report, the first step to minimizing the tax bite is to put your situation in focus. Estimate your gross income for this year and next. Tot up your exemptions and deductions. "If there are any sizable differences between the two years," urges the publishing concern, "look for ways to equalize."

That can be done by shifting more of your deductions into the higher tax year, or moving more of the income into the lower tax year. Salaried individuals don't have quite the same strategic options in shifting income as do professionals or those in business for themselves. They can move dollars around by either speeding up or slowing down the billing process. Income cannot be deferred, however, simply by neglecting to pick up a paycheck or two until after the start of a new year. Anything paid in a given year is taxable in that year.

Almost everyone, on the other hand, has at least some leeway on timing deductions, particularly charitable and medical deductions. If this has been a particularly good year for you, why not double up on the payments you've pledged to your church or college construction fund? It used to be that pre-paid interest charges could be written off in their entirety, but that escape hatch was sealed off when Congress ruled interest payments could be deducted only on a pro-rata basis over the life of the loan. New homeowners, however, can still deduct "points"— additional up-front interest charges paid on a mortgage—entirely in the year in which they were paid.

There is some discretion with estimated state income tax payments. They can be timed—pushed forward or delayed—to give you maximum advantage on the Federal return. Medical and dental expenses are usually fairly flexible, too. You can't deduct a pre-payment on some vague bill that's likely to come up in the future—a routine physical exam, for example.

But if you're undergoing an expensive course of dentistry, there are often times when it's advantageous to lump your payments in one year or another. You can deduct medical expenses only to the extent that they exceed 3 percent of adjusted gross income.

The 3 percent barrier can have an important bearing on whether you pay your bills in December of the current year, or in January of the next.

Assume for the sake of this discussion that you've got an adjusted gross income of $30,000 and that late this year, your dentist bills cost you $500. Your other medical expenses are only $200. "If you can," advises a Prentice-Hall report on year-end tax tactics, "pay in January of next year. You will get no deduction in this year anyway (3 percent of $30,000 is $900). So defer the expense until next year when you have a chance of exceeding the 3 percent floor."

Marital deductions can be timed, too. It may seem like rather a cold-blooded approach to the sacrament, but the income-splitting feature of filing a joint return is a grace note. Above the lowest bracket, it's the equivalent of a rate cut. Thus, if you're getting married next year, think about deferring income until then and accelerate deductions into this year.

If you've really made a killing this year—a big bonus, a lot of overtime, or even a sizable gain in the stock market—income averaging may help. Averaging cushions the bite of the graduated tax. It permits you to compute this year's tax as if the income had been spread equally over this year and the preceding four years. The option is open only if this year's taxable income is at least $3,000 more than 120 percent of the average for the preceding four years.

The key to intelligent tax planning—and the main line of defense against an I.R.S. audit—is good record keeping. The backbone of the system is original documents: earnings statements, vouchers, canceled checks. A good running record of outgo is essential to your overall financial plan, anyway. How else can you manage your spending unless you know what you're spending your money on? That same running record will make it easier for you to tell whether you should just take the standard deduction when you start doing the spadework on your income tax return, or whether you should itemize.

Try it both ways. In some years, it might be to your advantage to take the standard deduction with the idea that you'll push deductibles forward into the next year when you could be better off filing an itemized return. "As a rule," notes a Bank of America consumer information report, "you are likely to benefit by itemizing if during the tax year you have paid interest on a home loan, property taxes, or large unreimbursed medical bills; given large amounts to charity; or had major casualty or theft losses."

In addition to these obvious deductions, here are some others on which you should keep good documentation, as enumerated by the Bank of America:

● Business Use of Your Car. A log is essential. It should detail mileage, list the business purpose of each trip, and include receipts for such costs as gas, oil, repairs, garage rental, and registration costs.

● Donations. Most people hang on to the canceled checks needed to establish a charitable contribution, but many fail to keep records (an appraisal, for example) on the fair market value of property they have donated—old clothing or furniture. You can also deduct such out-of-pocket costs as automobile expenses you've run up while working for a charity. Keep a log on them, too.

- Sales Taxes. Many people just shrug their shoulders and take the standard formula deduction. If you're buying a lot of big ticket items in a given year, however—furnishing a home or an apartment, for example—keep your sales slips ready to hand. You may be entitled to a considerably larger deduction than the tax tables allow.

- Investment Expenses. Keep tabs on the money you have spent on financial publications, advisory services, the cost of renting the safety deposit box in which you store your securities. Even the transportation costs of a visit to your broker's office are deductible, if the trip involves discussion of a specific possibility.

Documentation is crucial in the very sensitive area of business entertainment expenses. The New York Society of Certified Accountants notes that "thousands of taxpayers lose perhaps millions of dollars in legitimate deductions each year simply because they are unable to document their expenditures, or have lost records that would remind them that deductible expenses were incurred."

Solid documentation is the only way to beat off an I.R.S. audit. The audit process is almost invariably a painful one. Almost 70 percent of all those audited have to pay more money, and only 8 percent get any money back. A recent sampling by the U.S. Comptroller General's office of 1,200 taxpayers who had been audited repeatedly showed they had to pony up an average $955 in additional charges and penalties. That compared with only $770 for all audits and resulted in a return of $178 per examiner hour, compared with $140 an hour on all audits.

Those numbers support the inference that the I.R.S. is as zealous in getting more bang for the buck as any businessman. The Government agency concentrates on auditing returns that will bring in the most money for the amount of time spent. Only about 4 percent of all returns get audited. But the chances are very high that if you get audited once, you are likely to be audited again. If you get into a bind like that, it's easy to feel that you're being picked on.

Draw whatever comfort you can from the Comptroller General's finding that there's no particular bias in the system—nothing "that would result in a particular return being audited year after year." There was "no indication," the Comptroller General continued, "that the I.R.S. repeatedly selected taxpayers for audit unless their returns indicated a probable tax change."

The taxpayers highest on the I.R.S. hit list tend to be people in business for themselves and professionals. Farmers (or individuals reporting some farm income) appear to have an only slightly lower priority. In most cases, the challenges zero in on two main areas— write-offs on unallowable expenses, and head of household claims that may not bear up under scrutiny.

To qualify for the lower head of household rate, a taxpayer has to be single or legally separated on Dec. 31 and have paid more than half the cost of maintaining the principal home of a relative or foster child.

The I.R.S. has found that too many individuals are trying to sneak phantom relatives onto the payroll.

Many other taxpayers get zapped for taking deductions that cannot legally be written off, or because they victimized themselves with their own sloppy record keeping. The preliminary audit signals really begin to flash red when the I.R.S. computers pick up a deduction that looks unusually high in relation to income. That's one reason why it helps to know what the averages are, as detailed in a study by Prentice-Hall (*see table below*).

AVERAGE DEDUCTIONS IN RELATION TO INCOME

Adjusted Gross Income		Contributions	Interest	Taxes	Medical	Total
$ 9,000 -	10,000	381	1,163	872	833	3,249
10,000 -	15,000	404	1,274	1,067	570	3,315
15,000 -	20,000	468	1,539	1,446	506	3,959
20,000 -	25,000	533	1,679	1,793	438	4,443
25,000 -	30,000	683	1,849	2,215	413	5,160
30,000 -	50,000	929	2,368	2,790	499	6,586
50,000 -	100,000	2,006	3,940	5,263	687	11,896
100,000	or more	9,946	10,445	13,001	1,057	34,449

Source: Prentice-Hall

An "average" looking return carries no particular magic. Trying to pass as average is no guarantee that you won't be flagged for audit. Nor should you have any hesitation in taking legitimate deductions, even if they seem larger than the norm. The I.R.S. computer programming has no particular claim to perfection, and in fact goes off half-cocked about 30 percent of the time, according to the Comptroller General's findings.

The I.R.S. is trying to shake some of the bugs out of the system. Further refinement should mean that fewer absolutely clean returns will be earmarked for audit, but plenty of taxpayers should clean up their act, too. Many of them get audited year after year because they go right on reporting the same unallowable items year after year.

Still others get themselves in hot water, innocently enough, by having their returns done by "unscrupulous preparers"—supposed professionals who have signed their names to returns on which unsupported deductions keep turning up.

There are plenty of sub-professional tax preparers around. Barber shops and real estate office windows all over the country blossom with their signs every year when tax time rolls around. More than four out of every 10 taxpayers get someone else to do their returns for them, at prices that range from under $10 to thousands. The level of skills varies widely, too—from the most untutored freelancer to the loftiest of the Big Eight accounting firms. Where to go?

I.R.S. officials say the big problem is the fly-by-nighter who sets up shop in a vacant storefront one tax year and is gone the next. "Always make sure you're dealing with someone who has a track record," urges one agency official.

Some consumer groups argue that only individuals with complicated tax problems should look for outside help. Their suggestion: try the I.R.S.

The Government agency offers a number of services

at no cost whatever. For those persistent souls who need only a bit of machete work in cutting through the jungle of form 1040, there is always the telephone. The toll-free number for your local district office is in the telephone book under the heading of U.S. Government.

If you need more than just juice and a couple of aspirins, why not make an office visit? Walk-ins are welcome. You get almost step-by-step advice from an I.R.S. auditor or field agent, but you have to do the pencil work on your own.

If you want to, you can drop the whole bloody mess into the I.R.S. bureaucratic lap. With the short form (1040A), all you need do is fill in such pertinent information as name, address, Social Security number, occupation, number of dependents, wages, dividends and interest. You have to fill in the amount of income tax withheld, too. The I.R.S. will do the figuring.

The procedure is the same with the 1040 long form, except that you cannot itemize deductions. You have to go along with the standard 16 percent deductions. So long as the package is in the I.R.S. hands before the April 15 deadline for filing, the agency will do all of the arithmetical dog work. Depending on how the bottom line looks, the I.R.S. will either send you a refund or bill you for the amount due.

For more detail on how the farm-out process works, see "Your Federal Income Tax," available free at I.R.S. offices, post offices and many banks well in advance of the mid-April day of wrath.

Auditors and field agents who work in the district offices are friendly enough; and patient, too, under circumstances that would often try the patience of the Great Accountant himself. Their help is servicable enough, but by comparison with what is generally available in private practice, a little rough-hewn. It falls short of the sophisticated—and quite legitimate—tax avoidance work that is the private practitioner's stock in trade. "It's not so much that a private practitioner will manipulate the figures for you as to tell you what to do—or avoid doing—next year," says an I.R.S. official.

From the outside looking in, it's hard for a layman to get a very good fix on just how sophisticated a private practitioner is. Word of mouth is often the best guide. If you don't like the results, you can always switch to someone else next year. One test of quality is whether the accountant is licensed to practice before the I.R.S. Earning the right to do so requires passing a tough two-day exam. That's not a complete test, but it is one hallmark that separates achievers from the amateurs.

Many privately owned chain preparers tend to draw some of their help from the ranks of what might be called semi-achievers—business and accounting students who still have a way to go before graduation. How good are the chains? Their quality seems to vary from office to office. One consumer group—the Ralph Nader Tax Reform Group—has argued that the accuracy of outside professionals on an itemized return is no better than the level of work done by I.R.S.

staffers. The chains, of course, contend that they do very good work indeed. In general, accounting skills are no different than anything else. You get what you pay for.

TOP DOLLAR TIPS

(1)   Everything you earn—and a lot of what you spend—has tax implications. Think ahead.

(2)   Timing is important. Shift income and deductions into one tax year or another whenever you can do so to your advantage.

(3)   If you've got a particularly big chunk of income in one year, try income averaging.

(4)   The best line of defense against an I.R.S. audit is a good set of records. Canceled checks, vouchers and diaries are all very much to the point.

Chapter 25

INCORPORATING

If you're wondering about the letters "P.C." or "P.A." that have suddenly blossomed after all the other capitals that follow your doctor's name, regard them as just one more sign of the times. They stand for Professional Corporation or Professional Association, and they mean that your physician is doing everything he can to keep himself healthy financially.

It's a rare professional or any other independent businessman these days who hasn't at least fantasized about the possibility of incorporating. It's easy to understand why. An initial investment of a few thousand dollars—often far less—in legal and incorporation fees can return many times that amount every year in a rich harvest of tax savings and plummy insurance, medical and retirement benefits.

Agreeable as those benefits are, there are defensive reasons for every entrepreneur to consider the possibility of incorporating, too. From the rise of the great trusts like Standard Oil in the last century to the full flowering of this century's conglomerates, businessmen have known all too well that they have a lot to lose. If you're in business for yourself, borrow money and can't pay it back, the lender has the right to attach anything in sight until he's made whole.

It's not just your frankfurter stand that's in jeopardy, but your house, your car, your savings and any other tangible asset the lender can find. If you're running a business as a sole proprietor or as a partnership, your head is on the block if anything goes wrong. Operating through a corporation, on the other hand, your personal liability is limited only to the amount of capital you put into the venture.

"Limited liability," says Eli Mason, senior partner in Mason & Co., a well-known accounting firm in New York City, "is by ten lengths the most important reason for incorporating."

That sort of protection can be important, and it may be reason enough to be born again as a corporation, even if the tax advantages don't work all your way. You have to look at the thing in context. Incorporation is not a panacea. The tax leverage really doesn't become significant until net income starts nudging $25,000 a year. But a corporation, if it is to survive I.R.S. scrutiny, requires more than a slap-dash modicum of record keeping.

The record keeping—and the financial planning that goes with it—can become a real burden for partners who decide to go the corporate route. When the proceeds of a partnership are divvied up, each of the partners takes the money and runs. Each decides on his own how much of his own share to earmark for insurance, investments, or a retirement program. In a corporation, it's group think. The officer-stockholders have to agree *en bloc* how the allocations are going to be made.

Thus, it might be a very sticky business to balance the wishes of an older physician for heavier contributions to the pension plan against the wishes of younger colleagues to plow more of the corporation's earnings back into new equipment, or a new office building. A corporation, precisely because it is a more complicated organism, demands more care and feeding than a proprietorship or a partnership. The care and feeding, of course, represent time and money. Are the trade-offs significant enough to make the difference?

This is a must question to thrash out with your accountant and/or lawyer before deciding whether or not to take the plunge. As Eli Mason notes, however, the potential tax savings can be very alluring. The first $25,000 of corporate earnings is levied at 17 percent and the next $25,000 at 20 percent. Personal income rates are scaled much higher. An individual who makes $50,000 is "way up there," says Mr. Mason.

The damages? Both single and married persons with $50,000 worth of earned income—after the standard deductions and exemptions—are in the 50 percent bracket. Up to $50,000, in fact, the corporate rate is substantially less than the personal rate. At the far end of the earnings scale, the individual is really between the rock and a hard place. The maximum corporate rate is 46 percent. The maximum personal rate on earned income is 70 percent.

The maximum rates tend to overstate the case, although they are bad enough to need no rhetorical ruffles and flourishes. With any sort of planning at all, no individual is likely to have all his income taxed in the top bracket. The incentive of the corporate shelter, however, is not to be denied. True, corporate dividends get taxed twice—once as corporate income, and then again as personal income. It is also true, however, that the two taxes you might have to pay as a corporate entrepreneur may be a lot less than the single tax you would pay as a sole proprietor.

For the sake of this discussion, let's assume that you're single and that you've got $40,000 worth of taxable income. That leaves you with a tax liability of $13,190. Now take a look at the same numbers from the corporate side. Assume you'd left $20,000 of that income in the corporation and taken the other $20,000 as salary. The corporation's liability would be $3,400 ($20,000 x 17 percent). Your personal liability on the balance would be $3,999. The total tax would be the sum of those numbers, or $7,399.

That represents a substantial saving—a kind of textbook demonstration of the magnitude of the tax savings a corporation can offer. Like most textbook demonstrations, the example suffers from an overdose of simplicity. The presumption is that an individual in the $40,000 bracket would be able to find ways of writing off more—a lot more—than just the zero bracket deduction. The example also presumes a yes answer to what is a totally subjective judgment. Would you be willing—or able, taking life style into account—to cut your $26,810 take home pay as an individual to the $16,101 you would take home as a corporate pooh-bah, just for the sake of an $8,400 tax saving? On paper, the potential savings are there. Whether they are there in the real world is something that should be explored in depth.

The name of the game is shape the corporation so that it does with pre-tax dollars what you are now doing for yourself with after-tax dollars. For example, you can quite legitimately capitalize on one very useful loophole—reimbursement plans under which the corporation agrees to take over the responsibility for the medical bills of key employees and their families.

Setting up such an agreement requires little more than formal approval of the board of the directors. All you have to do is put in your medical bills and the corporation pays you back. The reimbursement does not count as income. Things get a little more sticky outside the realm of the one- and two-man corporation, however. Part of the test is whether the beneficiary provides a substantial service to the corporation. A passive investor who holds stock in the company but does no real work for it is out of the running for what is in effect a double-barreled tax break. The corporation, like an individual, can write off the medical expenses as a tax deduction, but it has considerably more leeway in doing so. Individuals can begin taking the deduction only after the cost of medicine and drugs and direct medical costs exceed one percent and three percent, respectively, of adjusted gross income. The corporation, bound by no such restrictions, can take it all off.

Similar perks, within limits, are to be had in life and disability insurance. Key corporate employees are entitled to free life coverage on a one-year term basis up to a maximum of $50,000. The premiums are a deductible item for the corporation, and count as income to the employee only if the $50,000 ceiling is breached. There is no ceiling on disability protection, but the level of coverage should bear some reasonable relation to pay scales.

The list of goodies can go on and on. Assuming you've got cash flow enough to support all the glitter and can document solid business reasons for their presence on the property sheet, there is no reason why you can't put the corporate logo on such big ticket items as car and chauffeur, or even the latest in Lear Jets. You have to be in a position to establish, of course, that the hardware is ordinary and necessary to the pursuit of business. On a more mundane level, you can line up far richer pension benefits through a corporate plan than the $7,500 maximum allowable on the individual entrepreneur's best bet, a Keogh Plan.

Another big incentive to check out the pros and cons of incorporation is the tax-sheltered use you can make of retained earnings. Again within limits that bear some reasonable relation to the size of the business, you can allow earnings to pile up in the corporation without the I.R.S. asking too many questions. The profits do get taxed as earnings in the first instance, but they need not be plowed back immediately into inventory, equipment, or bricks and mortar.

Some of the cash, in fact, might well be invested in common stocks or perhaps even better yet, high yielding preferred stocks. Corporations pay taxes on only 15 percent of the dividends they receive.

Accumulations in excess of $150,000 that are not clearly earmarked for a definite business purpose are liable to tough penalties. If you're not careful about how the surplus piles up, you might even run afoul of the prohibition against personal holding companies—corporations owned by five or fewer individuals in which 60 percent or more of adjusted gross income comes from such "passive" sources as dividends, income, capital gains, royalties and annuities.

Not that a highly portable portfolio of stocks and Governments is such a bad thing to have tucked away in a corporation you might be thinking of folding about the time you plan to go into retirement. All such holdings are as good as cash, and generally easier to liquidate than inventory. There are several routes to take when you unwind a corporation, and most of them offer the prospect of low capital gains tax rates. On the other hand, if you want to sell the operation as a going business or pass it on to your heirs, incorporation can make for an easy transition. "Corporations," says Eli Mason, "need never die. They can continue in perpetuity." As a legal person, a corporation can truly be an extension of your own person.

A lot has been said about the ease with which the entrepreneur can dispense with legal advice in setting up a corporation. Can you really do it yourself? I personally would not make such a move without taking on all of the lawyerish and accounting help I could afford. But for two cogently written books on the other side of that argument, try Judith H. McQuown's *Inc. Yourself* (Macmillan Publishing Co., New York, 1977) and Ted Nicholas' *How to Form Your Own Corporation Without a Lawyer for Under $50* (Enterprise Publishing Co., 501 Beneficial Building, Wilmington, Del. 19801).

TOP DOLLAR TIPS

(1) Incorporation limits your personal liability, but probably won't generate any significant tax savings until net income is around the $25,000 mark.

(2) Corporate record keeping can be time-consuming and incorporation might cause conflicts that would never have cropped up in a partnership. Are the trade-offs meaningful enough for you to take the corporate plunge?

(3) If you incorporate, be sure to formalize the terms under which the corporation will provide such perks as medical reimbursement plans and life insurance.

(4) Be careful about the level of such passive income as dividends, interest and rent. Falling afoul of the personal holding company prohibitions could be costly.

Chapter 26

A RETIREMENT PLAN

If you're thinking these days about retirement in the same woolly, abstract way you did when you were 20—as something that happens to older people—you better sharpen your focus. Thanks to a high standard of living and a high level of medical care, retirement is as inevitable as liver spots for most of us. It is a state that deserves thinking about if only because of the ferocity with which inflation is snapping at our heels.

Extrapolating figures provided by the Bureau of Labor Statistics, the Bowery Savings Bank estimates that as recently as 1967 a retired couple could live in "moderately comfortable circumstances" on about

$3,600 a year. It now takes around $7,000 to maintain that same bare-bones minimum expectation life style. Ten years from now? Twenty years from now? Who knows? Assuming a constant annual inflation rate of 6 percent, the Bowery projects that same couple will need $24,000 a year to get by in 1999.

An awesome number, but getting there is half the fun. One way to make the journey is with the help of those two great middle-class tax shelters—a Keogh Plan or an Individual Retirement Account.

Both work essentially the same way. They permit you to deduct a certain amount of money from your earnings, tax-free, and tuck it into one or another savings or investment vehicles. The interest or dividends paid on the cash multiplies tax-free until you are ready to retire at age 59½ or later. Both principal and interest are taxable as ordinary income when you begin to draw the money down, but your tax bracket will presumably be lower in retirement than in your peak earning years. Thus, Keogh Plans and I.R.A. (pronounced like the man's name) offer not the grace of tax forgiveness, but tax deferral.

Though much the same in their mechanics, the programs differ in major respects. Keogh Plans are open only to the self-employed and their employees. They are much favored by professionals, but have also found a big market among moonlighters—journalists who free lance, and teachers who are also part-time sales reps, for example.

I.R.A.s, on the other hand, are open only to people not covered by a pension or profit sharing plan where they work, employers who don't want to provide a pension plan for employees (as they must with a Keogh), and otherwise unemployed housewives whose husbands are not covered by a pension plan where they work. The Keogh Plan has broader boundaries. It permits you to shelter 15 percent of your annual net income, up to a maximum of $7,500 each year. The same 15 percent applies to I.R.A.s, but the ceiling—an annual maximum of $1,500—is much lower.

The I.R.A., however, does carry one new dazzling raised-consciousness wrinkle—a provision explicitly designed to recognize the value of the services provided in the home by a non-working spouse of either sex. Until recently, a husband could make his wife the beneficiary of his I.R.A., but it was hers only if he died. Joint accounts were illegal and the account was the sole property of the person who opened it.

Now a working spouse can open an I.R.A. for the better half at home. There is an extra cash incentive to do so in the form of a slightly larger tax deduction—a total of $1,750 instead of the standard $1,500.

Congress has stipulated, though, that the annual contribution, whatever its size, must be split evenly between the two separate accounts. Each can make the other a beneficiary, but the cash deposited to the credit of a non-working spouse is, as one banker put it, "irrecoverably hers." Is the extra $250 deduction incentive enough for a spouse to give away $875, no strings attached? Listen to Earl McGuire, Jr., a top official of the Bank of Asheville, N.C., and former chairman of the American Bankers Association Committee on Investment Retirement Accounts. "I think it all depends on the marriage," he says. "If it's a solid marriage and the husband wants his wife to have some protection in her own name, I would think he'd jump at the chance."

Savings banks, savings and loan associations, commercial banks and mutual funds have all jumped at the marketing chance they've been given by I.R.A.s and Keoghs. All such plans must be trusteed. It's the law. It's possible, but a mite cumbersome and expensive, to design a package for yourself. It's much simpler—and cheaper—to enroll in one administered by a financial institution that has already gone to the trouble of getting I.R.S. approval of its master plan.

Where you put your I.R.A. or Keogh money is mainly a question of temperament and investment objective. The bulk of the money filters into high-yielding bank certificates of deposit, but insurance company annuities are growing in popularity. The least popular alternatives are mutual funds and 6 percent United States Retirement Bonds—the former because of the level of risk involved, the latter because better returns can be found elsewhere along the yield curve. It is possible to set up more than one I.R.A. or Keogh. If you were willing to accept some risk in the hope of blunting the hammer blows of inflation, for example, you might put one dollar into a mutual fund for every two dollars you put into certificates.

If you do opt for a non-bank alternative—an annuity or a mutual fund—be wary of up-front sales charges that will bite into your return. The size of that bite is particularly important, the Federal Trade

Commission warned recently, on I.R.A. annuity plans that require fixed payments over a number of years. Many insurance companies deduct sales and administrative charges in the early years of the contract. The charges are not refundable if you can't keep up the payments, and that could very easily happen if your income drops.

Suppose you're making $10,000 a year. You want to take the full 15 percent allowed you, so you open a fixed payment I.R.A. with $1,500. The next year your income falls to $8,000. Since you can now make only a maximum payment of $1,200 there is no way you can cover the $1,500 bogey you contracted to cover. "In such instances," the U.S. Office of Consumer Affairs cautions, "an I.R.A. holder may lose a significant portion of his . . . investment because of cancellation penalties imposed by insurance companies for not meeting the fixed payment schedule."

I.R.A.s and Keoghs are not all gravy. You can't invade the principal or interest of a plan without a stiff penalty. If the money comes out before you reach age 59½, except in the case of death or disability, it gets taxed as ordinary income and is subject to a 10 percent surcharge as well. If the cash is in a time deposit, you are also vulnerable to the interest penalties the banks ordinarily levy on premature withdrawals.

The lash of the bank penalty also makes it difficult to take advantage of the "rollover" provisions of I.R.A. You're allowed to shift your cash from one investment plan to another every three years. In a period of rising interest rates, for example, it would be very nice to be able to move your money with them—out of an 8 percent certificate, say, into one carrying a 10 percent rate. The disincentive of the penalty all but forces you to stay put with the money you've already got in the bank. You could stick to short maturities, but the rates on them are generally lower anyway.

There is considerably more flexibility with the I.R.A.'s other rollover privilege. That is the right to take any lump sum pension settlement you get— either because you're leaving for another job or because the pension plan has been terminated—and put it into an I.R.A. without regard to the $1,500 limit. That can be done without tax liability so long as you set up the plan within 60 days of having got the lump sum. The account should be kept separate from your other I.R.A. money. Keeping it segregated allows you to roll the cash back into a corporate pension plan, again without tax liability, if you should happen to go to work for another company that has a retirement program.

Whether or not you've been able to work an I.R.A. or a Keogh into your retirement strategy, your planning should include a realistic assessment of what your income and expenses will be after you get the golden handshake. How much of a company pension can you expect? Explore the options. Will the payoff be significantly better if you hang around beyond age 65? What are the rights of survivorship? What do the actuarial tables look like? Is your wife/husband so much younger that she/he is likely to survive you by a number of years? If so, are you willing to accept a somewhat lower pension now as a trade-off against payments that will continue after your death?

Keep tabs on what you will draw from Social Security. The level of payments keeps changing all the time. To keep current, drop by your local Social Security office and pick up a copy of the free pamphlet "Estimating Your Social Security Retirement Check." Remember that you must be at least 62 before Social Security starts paying off.

You ought to file for Social Security two or three months before you retire. That means a trip to a Social Security office in person. Bring along your Social Security number, your spouse's and the date of your marriage; a copy of last year's income tax return or your form W2, and a certified copy of your birth certificate or baptismal certificate.

After you've got a good fix on the cash flow you can expect from your pension, Social Security, dividends, interest and any other source of income you have, project your expenses. Income taxes will almost certainly be lower. Your commuting and clothing costs are likely to be lower, too. Unless you are very lucky, affluent or both, it is unlikely that your retirement income will match what you have been making.

Thus, it's a good idea to cut your fixed costs wherever you can. Try not to go into retirement with a lot of debt outstanding. Check out your investment portfolio. Post-retirement is the time to start considering shifting out of low-yielding stocks you may have bought for their growth prospects into something that produces a little more income. If interest rates are up, maybe the move should be into bonds.

Get a thorough physical six months before you retire. If it turns up anything troublesome that might be fixed up by elective surgery, for example, maybe you should have the job done while you've still got plenty of corporate sick time to burn. What kind of medical insurance will you be able to take with you? If you can't stay on as part of the group, start shopping for some kind of replacement coverage well before you leave.

You will automatically be covered by Medicare at age 65 if you've been collecting Social Security benefits. It's generally a good idea to take (at a small monthly fee) the so-called Part B supplementary Medicare. You are automatically included in Part B, which covers physicians' services, unless you specifically opt out. Part A covers "in hospital" care. Medicare is not a complete package. The deductibles and co-insurance features of the plan keep rising all the time, in train with medical costs generally. Look into the "Medigap" policies provided by private health insurance carriers. Blue Cross and Blue Shield account for almost two-thirds of all such complementary insurance sold. Many companies will not cover anyone who did not get on the books before age 65, and even a complementary policy doesn't do the entire job.

No matter what the coverage, you will still have to meet on your own the cost of routine health care, doctor's fees that exceed Medicare reimbursement allowances, and the cost of custodial care in a convalescent hospital. Count on routine health items, including dental care, to cost a retired couple in excess of $500 a year.

Check out your life insurance policies. Most companies permit retirees to convert at least a portion of their group coverage to one or another form of individual policy at the standard rate for your age group. How much life insurance will you really need in retirement? Far less, certainly, than when you still had the children to put through college. If you've got a permanent policy, perhaps you can borrow against it and get a better return on the cash value elsewhere. Alternatively, you can use the cash value to buy some paid-up coverage or an annuity that will generate some income.

Like many looking down the road to retirement, you ought to consider the possibility of continuing to work part-time for a while; partly because doing so will stretch your cash income, partly because a job might add to your psychic income as well. There are limits to the amount of paid employment you can take on and still keep all of your Social Security. You can check those limits out with a phone call to your nearest Social Security office.

The trend is definitely to work, even among well-heeled corporate executives. Look at the results of a survey of 3,800 upper echelon managers and professionals done recently by the Conference Board, a business supported research organization. The 3,800 retired between 1961 and 1976. By this time last year, more than half of the group was still working part-time—either for pay, or as vŏlunteers.

Most of those working for money, the Conference Board found, were working for themselves, mainly in one-man shops operating in fields totally unrelated to their former jobs. The reach is a broad one, ranging from farming and truck driving to real estate brokerage.

The study was directed by Walter S. Widstrom of the Conference Board. He found that "one of the most striking aspects of the survey was the participants' nearly-unanimous feeling that a satisfying retired life hinges on keeping busy." For most of the people in the study, keeping busy meant "meaningful work."

What you will do in retirement is partly a function of where you plan to live. That question requires a lot of thinking about to resolve, too. Many people reach for what they hope will be better climates—or cheaper ones—only to find the quicksilver flash of illusion has shot through their hands.

Here, as detailed by the Citicorp publication *Consumer Views*, are some of the most important things to look into before making the leap to a new post-retirement home.

● Housing. Thoroughly research prices and rents. There is no substitute for on-the-spot legwork—done, perhaps, on a couple of pre-retirement vacations. One useful library source, though, is the *National Directory on Housing for Older People*, available at this writing for $2.50 from the National Council on the Aging, 1828 L Street, N.W., Washington, D.C. 20036.

● Taxes. Many states offer substantial tax concessions to older people, concessions that may well have an important bearing on where you decide to establish your principal residence. Send for the free 73-page booklet "Tax Facts" available from the American Association of Retired Persons, 1909 K Street, N.W., Washington, D.C. 20049.

● The quality of health care. How does the area stack up against others in terms of doctors and number of hospital beds? Check that information through the County or State Medical Association.

● Climate. Climatic studies on most cities and states are available from the National Climatic Center, Federal Building, Asheville, N.C. 28801.

● Recreational and cultural facilities. Interested in golf, concerts, painting? Try the local Chamber of Commerce. Most states also have, generally located in the capital city, a treasure trove of information that goes under the rubric of the Department of Aging or the Council on Aging. Use its resources to help you tie down loose ends.

A lot can be learned about prices, zoning and tax problems by subscribing to the local papers for a while. Above all, the Citicorp consumer advisers caution, don't pack up and move "until you've visited the place and stayed for as long as you can manage." "Visit markets, neighborhoods; talk to as many people who live there as you can," the advisers continue. "Get around by public transportation. Imagine you are there for keeps. How does it feel?"

Estate planning—making sure that your assets will go where you want them to go with a minimum of tax liability and administrative liability—is also very much part of the pre-retirement drill. Are there tax advantages to be gained by assigning your life insurance policies to your spouse, or by shifting some of your assets into a trust of one kind or other? Talk it over with your accountant and lawyer.

And if you haven't had your will checked in the last couple of years, do so now. Wholesale revisions of the law, among other things, made sweeping changes in the way jointly owned property is treated.

Major changes in circumstances—such as the advent of retirement—should prompt a review of your will, too. What about your executor, or the guardian you might have named for your dependent children? Are they still willing to take on that responsibility, or have they reached a stage in their own lives when they'd just as soon pass the torch on to someone else?

If you don't have a will—maybe because you don't like the idea of contemplating your own mortality—now is the time to have one put together. The cost is modest, maybe $75 and up for a comparatively uncomplicated one. Why leave a vacuum behind you, or go through retirement with the uneasy feeling that you've left something important undone? That observation holds true for your finances generally. Make a plan, set some objectives, ask tough questions of anyone who tries to sell you a financial service, whether it's auto insurance, a combined savings and checking account, or an interesting looking emerging growth company. You really don't need a couple of years at the Harvard Business School to make your money work harder than you do.

TOP DOLLAR TIPS

(1) Start planning for retirement now—the earlier, the better. Are you eligible for an I.R.A. or a Keogh Plan?

(2) Can you compound the advantages of an I.R.A. by setting up an account for your spouse, too?

(3) Cut your fixed costs before going into retirement. If you've got a lot of debt hanging over you, start whittling it down to manageable proportions in the years before retirement.

(4) Find out how much and what kind of medical insurance you can take with you into retirement well before you leave the job. If need be, sign up for supplementary coverage as much as a year or two before you get the golden handshake.

GLOSSARY

Add on interest rates. Loan in which total interest charges are superimposed on amount borrowed. Similar to discount loan. In both cases, the effective rate of interest is roughly twice the simple rate.

Adjusted balance, average adjusted daily balance, balance after deduction. All methods on which loan balances are computed. Adjusted balance is best for the consumer.

Annual Percentage Rate (APR). The true rate of interest charged on a loan, listed in boldface on application.

Bond. Promissory note issued by Federal Government and its agencies; by state and local governments; by corporations. State and local bonds ("municipals") are also known as tax-exempts because they are not liable to Federal income taxes. They are either general obligations, backed by local tax power; or revenue bonds, secured by income from a specific project. Corporate bonds are also often secured by a pledge of assets, and in any event have a first claim on the assets. A debenture is a bond secured only by the credit of the company.

Book Value. Corporate assets to which common stockholders have a pro-rata claim after the obligations of a debt and preferred holders have been paid off. Often used to describe the theoretical liquidating value of a company.

Callable. Term used to describe bonds or preferred stock that can be retired at the option of the corporation, usually at a premium.

Cash Flow. Net income plus depreciation. An important measure of a company's profitability and its ability to meet interest charges on debt.

Certificates of Deposit. Sometimes known as "C.D.'s." Issued by commercial banks and savings and loans for specific periods ranging from 90 days on out to 4 or more years at higher rates than those available on regular savings accounts. Rates on C.D.s of more than $100,000 are negotiable. Under that amount, rates are regulated by the Federal Reserve.

Closed-End. A form of investment company with a fixed number of shares outstanding, traded on either the New York or American Stock Exchanges or in the over-the-counter market.

Commercial Paper. Unsecured short term promissory note issued by corporations at rates generally higher than those available on Treasury bills.

Condominium. Dwelling unit owned outright by purchaser, who shares ownership of such common appurtenances as hallways, stairs, recreation areas.

Convertibles. A sub-species of bonds and preferred stocks that can be exchanged for common stock, and which generally carry less risk than direct stock ownership.

Co-op, co-operative apartment. Resident draws right to occupy from shares in common ownership of structure and appurtenances.

Cumulative Preferred. A form of preferred stock whose holders must be paid any omitted dividends that have piled up before any distribution can be made to common stockholders. *(See Preferred Stock below.)*

Debenture. *(See Bond above.)*

Discount. One of Wall Street's great portmanteau words. If a company's earnings jump and the stock doesn't move (or even sells off), the market is said to have "discounted" the news. Also applied to a bond that is trading below par, a stock that is trading below book value, or the shares of a closed-end investment company trading below net asset value.

Dividend Payout. A measure of how much of a company's earnings are being paid to shareholders and, conversely, what percentage of profits is being plowed back into the business. A company that earns $2 a share and pays $1 a share in dividends has a payout ratio (1 divided by 2) of 50 percent. Its plowback ratio is also 50 percent.

E Bonds. U.S. Savings Bonds sold on a discount basis. An initial purchase of $18.75 brings $25 on maturity five years later, for an average annual return over that period of 6 percent. Must be distinguished from H bonds, which are sold in denominations of $500, pay 6 percent semi-annually, and mature in 10 years.

Equal Credit Opportunity Act. Forbids discrimination in lending. A woman can't be turned down for a loan just because she's a woman, or because she's married, single, separated, divorced or widowed.

Fair Credit Reporting Act.   Lender must supply prospective borrower who has been refused credit the reasons for the turn-down. Guarantees free access to information in credit agency files if requested within 30 days of loan rejection.

Federal Agency Securities.   Backed by moral obligation of U.S. Government and issued by such agencies as the Banks for Co-Operatives, the Federal Home Loan Banks and the Federal Land Banks, these debentures generally carry slightly higher yields than direct Treasury issues. They are exempt from state and local, but not Federal income taxes.

Flexible Loan Insurance Programs. These "FLIP" mortgages are a variation of graduated payment mortgage plans designed particularly for younger people. Monthly payments start at comparatively low level, gradually increase to a constant level as (one hopes) the income level of homebuyer increases.

Float.   Another portmanteau word. The credit that hangs up in the air from the point at which a check is written to the point at which it is presented for collection at the bank on which it is drawn. Also used to describe the number of shares in a company available for public trading after the holdings of officers, directors and other insiders have been subtracted from the total number outstanding.

Graduated Payment Mortgage.   Basis of such offshoots as FLIP mortgages (see above). Unlike FLIP, there is no escrow on down payment to supplement payments, and no mandatory use of private mortgage insurance.

Income Averaging.   Provision of tax code that takes some of the sting out of significant jump in income by treating the increase as if it had been spread over a period of five years.

Indexing. Investment technique which hopes to do no worse (and no better) than market as a whole by salting portfolio with proportionate amounts of the 500 or so major companies conceived to be "the market."

Individual Retirement Account. Permits individuals not covered by pension plan to deduct $1,500 or 15 percent of income, whichever is less, and contribute cash to a retirement account. Contribution is written off against gross income. Dividends or interest earned on contributions accumulates tax-free. (*See also Keogh Plan.*)

Investment Company. Invest in stocks, bonds, preferreds or some combination thereof, with income and/or capital gains passed on to holders of underlying shares. Most such companies are open-end—they continuously sell shares in themselves directly to investors and stand ready to redeem those shares at any time. Closed-end companies (see above) do neither. They are bought and sold in the auction markets rather than on a direct basis.

Kaffirs. South African gold shares, named after the Bantu who work the mines.

Keogh Plan. Tax-sheltered retirement plan for self-employed individuals, who are permitted to deduct up to 15 percent of net or $7,500—whichever is less—for contribution to program. (*See Individual Retirement Account above.*)

Leverage. Another portmanteau word, generally meant to describe situation in which the use of borrowed money can enhance return on investment—and multiply losses proportionately, if things don't work out. A corporation which carries a lot of debt is said to be heavily leveraged. So is an investment company that takes on debt as part of its investment strategy.

Limited Partnership. Structure common to most tax-shelter deals. Limited partners have no say in day-to-day operation of business and their liability, in case of financial difficulty, is limited to size of their cash contribution. In return for use of their capital, limited partners are entitled to major share of the return on their investment. Managing partner also shares in the profits.

Load–No-Load. Generally speaking, a sales charge levied on insurance, the purchase of unit trusts, certificates or open-end investment company shares. Mutual funds that do not carry such a charge are said to be no-load.

Money Market Fund. Open-end investment company which specializes in short term obligations like Treasury bills, certificates of deposit and commercial paper.

Municipal Bond Fund. Open-end investment company which specializes in tax-exempts. Interest payments from muni bond funds are tax-free. Capital gains are taxable at capital gains rate.

Mutual Fund. *(See Investment Company above.)*

Net Asset Value. Book value or net worth in the case of a corporation. In the case of an open- or closed-end investment company, the term is usually used to describe the market value of the portfolio in pro-rata relationship to each of the underlying shares. Think of a pie having a net asset value of $5. Each of its five slices would have a net asset value of $1 a share. If the shares were selling for 50 cents each, they would be trading at a discount of 50 percent.

Net Worth. Same as *book value (see above)*. But the term also describes what you are worth as an individual (materially speaking, of course) after you've subtracted all of your liabilities from your assets.

NOW Accounts. Stands for Negotiable Order of Withdrawal—in effect the checking accounts savings banks were empowered to offer on an experimental basis.

Open-End. Refers to investment companies (*see above*), but also to a line of credit where the monthly payments vary with billings—credit cards or department store charge accounts, for example.

Over-the-Counter. Describes the wildly variegated market in which dealers trade stocks and some bonds for themselves and their customers on a negotiated "bid and ask" basis. The dealers tend to specialize in issues, sometimes in as many as several hundred. The bid is the price at which the dealer is willing to buy from an investor; the asked price at which he is willing to sell. In an inactive issue, there may be a spread (a difference) of several points between those two prices. As distinguished from the negotiated OTC market, the New York Stock Exchange and the American Exchange are auction markets. Both cater to a much broader investment interest than the counter market, and prices are set by the continuous flow of buy and sell orders.

Par. In the case of a bond, face value—often $1,000. Bonds are usually quoted in terms of par. If you see 100 after a bond listing in the financial pages, it means the issue is selling for $1,000. Move the decimal one place to the right. A quote of 102½, for instance, means the bond is selling at $1,025. Preferreds are initially sold at "par," often but not always $100. Market value and par value are not the same thing—one can be less or more than the other. Common stocks used to be issued on a par basis of some kind, but most now come out no-par.

Points. Another portmanteau word. A lender might charge "points" (a point being 1 percent) as a one-time service charge on a mortgage. When a stock gains or loses a point, its price has changed by a dollar. When a bond gains or losses a point, its price has changed by $10.

Preferred Stock. Carries a fixed dividend, usually has no voting power, no maturity, and a higher claim on dividends than common stockholders. *(See Callable and Cumulative Preferred above.)*

Price-Earnings Ratio. A standard measure of how cheap or expensive a stock is in relation to the earning power behind it. A stock that sells for $10 a share and earns $2 a share is said to be trading at five times earnings.

Prime Rate. Interest charged the most credit-worthy blue chip corporate risks. Most other rates scale upward from the prime.

Private Mortgage Insurance. Coupled with conventional mortgages, P.M.I. often permits borrowers to get by with lower down payments on a house. It is generally used to cover the difference between a very low down payment (say 5 percent) and the larger down payment a lender would like to see (say 20 percent).

Random Walk. Theory that listed stock markets are so well-researched and so "efficient" that the price of a stock reflects everything known about it at the time. The corollary is that unless you've got some inside information, no one stock is any better a buy or sale than any other.

Redemptions. Cash-in of open-end investment company shares. When an open-end has to redeem more shares than it sells, the fund is said to be in redemption.

Return on capital/return on net worth. Standard analytical measures of profitability. The return on capital shows how much the company is making on all the money, including borrowed money, employed in the business. The return on net worth shows how much the company is making on the common stockholders equity in the business. When a company has a high debt ratio, return on capital is a more significant measure of profitability.

Return on Sales.   A standard analytical measure of profitability, which tends to vary from industry to industry. A company which nets $1 million on sales of $20 million has a return on sales (or profit margin) of 5 percent.

Rollover.   A tax-free event, such as the conversion of E bonds into H bonds; or the transfer of a lump sum pension payment into an I.R.A.

Round Lot.   Even units in which securities trade—100 shares for common stock, 10 shares for preferred stock, 10 bonds (or $10,000) for bonds. Commissions are always cheaper on round lots than on odd lots—any order that falls below the round lot definition.

Straight (Ordinary) Life Insurance.   Policy which accumulates cash and loan values, and on which premiums remain level after purchase. As distinguished from Term Insurance, which accumulates neither loan nor cash values, and on which premiums continue to rise with age.

Tax Shelter.   A form of investment—real estate syndication, oil and gas drilling—designed to minimize or defer tax liabilities.

Treasury Bill.   Short term obligation of U.S. Government, sold in denominations of $10,000 (and multiples of $5,000 thereafter at maturities ranging from 91 days to 1 year).

Unit Trusts.   A fixed pool of income securities (bonds or preferred stocks), generally fairly well diversified to minimize risk and produce the highest return possible, consistent with safety. Unit trusts are unmanaged, as distinguished from somewhat similar investment companies whose managers shift with the market in an effort to maximize returns.

Variable Rate Mortgages. Mortgages on which interest charges move up and down with money rates generally.

Yield. The current return on a security, computed by dividing annual dividend or interest payments by market price. A stock that pays $2 and sells for $20 carries a yield of 10 percent. In general, the higher the yield, the higher the risk.

INDEX

Greater New York Savings
Bank, 45
Growth-income funds, 191

H bonds, 28, 30
Herzfeld, Thomas J., 207, 208,
209, 211, 228
HH bonds, 28
Hirsch, Yale, 183–84, 189,
197, 254
*Hirsch Mutual Funds
Almanac, The*, 184
Holt, T. J., 194–95, 250
Holt Investment Advisory,
194–95, 250
Home financing, 129–40;
closing costs, 137–40;
down payment, 130–31;
FLIP mortgage, 136;
government, 132–33, 134;
G.M.P., 134–36; investment
strategy, 131–32; leverage,
132; P.M.I., 133–34
Home improvement loans,
144–45; deductible, 158;
importance of, 157–58
Homeowner's insurance,
156–59
Home value, 141–49;
appraisal, 145–46;
improvement loans,
144–45; refinancing the
mortgage, 141–44; tax bite
and, 146–48; tax exclusion,
146
Hospitalization coverage. *See*
Medical insurance
House hunting, 119–28;
checklist for, 123–24;
inspecting and inspection
costs, 126–28;
neighborhood renovations,
124–25; old houses and,
125–28; renting or buying,
120–24; speculative

trading, 120; supply and
demand, 119–20; tax
bracket factor, 121
*How to Form Your Own
Corporation Without a
Lawyer for Under $50*
(Nicholas), 284

Income funds, 191
Income tax management,
254–97; incorporation,
277–84; I.R.S. and,
265–76; retirement plan,
285–97; tax-exempt bonds,
247–55; tax shelters,
256–64
Income tax planning, 265–76;
auditor and field agent
help, 275–76; deductions,
266–70, 272; effectiveness
of, 266; filing deadline,
274; I.R.S. help, 273–75;
record keeping and
documentation, 268–71
Inc. Yourself (McQuown), 284
Individual Retirement
Account (I.R.A.), 286–89;
premature withdrawals,
289; "rollover" provisions
of, 289–90
Inflation, 3, 6, 68, 99, 125,
129, 157, 163, 173, 176,
219–20, 223, 235, 247, 288
Installment loans, 55
Insurance, 93–116;
homeowner's, 156–59;
medical and disability,
108–16; premiums, 121;
term policies, 93–107
Interest, savings account,
19–37; bank, 19–26;
bankers' acceptances, 34;
best deal, 24–25;
certificates of deposit, 34;
commercial paper, 34;

partly because a good chunk of the portfolio has been in equities as well as bonds, and partly because the fund's aggressive approach to trading profits has made for very high portfolio turnover. Operating costs, as a result, tend to be comparatively high and cut into yield. Tom Herzfeld, probably the specialist in closed-ends, argues that "there's no point" in buying an open-end bond fund when "you can buy just as good a portfolio through a closed-end at a discount." There is some merit to that argument.

Many of the open-end bond funds carry an 8 percent load charge that can reduce a smaller investor's effective yield considerably. The industry trend is towards no-load. If it's maximum current income you want, my feeling is that you're better off with a no-load. Bond funds have different objectives. The Keystone group, for example, has one fund that specializes in investment grade bonds, another which specializes in medium growth bonds, and still another that specializes in discount bonds.

Many bond funds try to soup up their total return (income plus appreciation) with a blend of high-to-medium and low grade bonds. Others shoot the moon with "junk" bonds, low grade deep-discount bonds. That category includes the Lord Abbett Bond-Debenture Fund, Keystone B-4, and the First Investors Fund for Income, among others. All such funds are riskier than their more conservative fellows, but they have proved extremely popular—as popular as the stream of direct junk underwritings yielding 12 percent and 13 percent that have lately been coming to market in heavy volume.

Some degree of diversification is as useful in bonds as in stocks, though the range need not be as broad. And diversification might be one reason for getting into the market through closed- or open-end bond funds rather than by direct investment.

Among the biggest closed-end bond funds you can track in the financial pages and Weisenberger (see Chapter 16), are American General Bond Fund, Drexel Bond-Debenture Trading Fund, John Hancock Investors, Inc., Montgomery Street Income Securities, and Mutual of Omaha Interest Shares. In all, there are 24 closed-end bond funds, most of which trade on the New York Stock Exchange.

Many of the closed-ends offer both good yields and often a way to buy bonds at a discount. The depth of the discounts varies with the state of the bond and stock markets. When both are down, the discounts deepen. The discounts also tend to vary with the portfolio quality. The conservatively managed American General Bond Fund, for instance, traded at a small premium for much of the period 1971-77, and then slipped to a small discount when interest rates seemed once again to be marching to historic highs. The fund has been upgrading a portfolio that was good to begin with. About 80 percent of assets were tucked into high quality debt, Government obligations, prime commercial paper and cash. The balance was a little more venturesome, but turnover was modest. All of that added up to a net asset value and a market price that moved pretty closely in train with each other.

Drexel Bond-Debenture, on the other hand, has sold at a discount of as much as 20 percent below asset value,